WISCONSIN CENTRAL

WISCONSIN CENTRAL

REGIONAL RAILROAD POWERHOUSE IN REVIEW

DEAN SAUVOLA

FONTHILL

Fonthill Media Inc.
www.fonthillmedia.com
office@fonthillmedia.com

First published 2023

ISBN 978-1-63499-482-8

Typeset in Mrs Eaves XL Serif Narrow
Printed and bound in England

FOREWORD

The Wisconsin Central has been the subject of many articles and excellent books through the years. It would be a tall order to improve on any of that work and likely redundant. Instead, my aim with this book is to look back on the railroad from a perspective a couple decades after the fact. For those who are learning about the WC for perhaps the first time, I have tried to condense and include the events that made the railroad a dynamic place in one volume. WC made a lot of news during its run, making this a formidable challenge; no doubt there are some omissions by necessity and worthy topics only touched upon in passing. To try and keep the focus on "WC territory," I have decided to include the effect of the Algoma Central purchase on WC without covering operations on that new subsidiary in Ontario. A lot of the equipment was used interchangeably across the border, and the Algoma Central would make a worthy subject on its own.

This book is in part a personal reflection on what fascinated me about the WC. As such, the narrative and photos reflect my take on this fallen flag. I have long been interested in how railroads meet the terrain they cross, connect communities, intersect with each other, and evolve over time. Photographing the WC was like watching these processes happen in fast forward. It seemed like there was always something about to change, be bought, a new connection made, old routes severed, new service instituted, or a new partnership for new traffic—a fun but frantic time. I am still amazed, even now, when seeing the work of others, aspects, operations, and details I had not caught at the time. I hope others find the same joy of discovery in this book, even if they spent time trackside during the WC era.

While I try to cover a lot of terrain that the WC covered, of course there are limitations. I will note one here: the south end of the Chicago Sub and its namesake city. Readers should not infer from the lack of Chicagoland connections coverage that I in any way downplay the importance of the railroad capital to the WC. Quite the opposite, it is my contention that without the unrestricted access WC had to make direct connections to other railroads, it would not have enjoyed the success that it did. The complexity of the carriers and connections in and around Chicago could be the basis for another WC book, material that would overwhelm this book. The way WC funneled most of its traffic to Chicago meant Shops Yard in North Fond du Lac functioned as its Chicago yard in a lot of ways. Each day, trains were blocked for numerous other railroads at Shops and sent over the Chicago Sub directly to the yards of other carriers in the Windy City (often reflected in foreign road run-through power). WC's own Schiller Park Yard was used for local work and transfers as well, but most of the interchange traffic was blocked at Shops and "transferred" long-distance to the other carriers at Chicago via time freights.

With the personal scope of this book, I drew from my collection of photography of the WC. I have had the good fortune to live in five different places while the WC was operating, all within a reasonable distance of the WC, some within eyeshot. Reflecting upon all the days spent photographing the WC during the different phases of my life has been a labor of love. The struggle was in selecting a group of images to best tell this complex story.

I would be remiss without a heartfelt thank you to my family, wife Rachel, daughters Abby and Iris, all the friends who have been part of my photographic adventures, and to all the friendly railroaders of the Wisconsin Central who provided a bounty of information, anecdotes, and insights through the years. Special thanks to Rudy Maki who reviewed this book ahead of its publication and has been a photographic mentor of mine for about as long as I have been wielding a camera.

CONTENTS

INTRODUCTION

The era of railroad building was considered over around 100 years ago when railroad barons were putting the finishing touches on vast empires. They were so successful at their elite art that they earned the moniker robber barons due to their ability to affect the travel and trade of the nation while amassing great fortunes. In the eyes of many, the age of railroad construction was over. While it is true that once the United States was built-out and developed into cities, towns, farms, and ranches, acquiring the vast strips of right-of-way upon which to build an empire became a large obstacle, I would argue that the railroad builders of our time constructed new empires by different means. Edward A. Burkhardt was one of the modern builders who drew upon a career in railroading to see opportunities around the Midwest (and later the world) among overlooked and cast-off routes. In leading the Wisconsin Central, he built a profitable railroad that altered the course of railroad history in Wisconsin and neighboring states. Constructing railroads in the regional era resulted in dynamic new systems, although they were built through strategic purchases and customer relationships, not the surveys and construction crews of a century before. The regional movement was nearly as significant, however, in setting the stage for the next century.

An earlier era of heavy regulation was displaced by a new age of dynamic competition and mergers in the wake of the Staggers Rail Act of 1980. The lessening of nearly 100 years of rules acknowledged the modern reality that competition outside of the industry, particularly trucking, meant railroads no longer had a shipping monopoly and needed additional agility to compete. Mergers and spinoffs were in full swing by the late 1980s, with railroad profitability on the upswing. This environment was fertile ground for a new railroad like the Wisconsin Central Ltd. Much of the WC's success was through innovation and partnerships with the shippers they served, thanks to the dedication of the employees at all levels of the company. The lines WC acquired were small enough to not be deemed major transactions by the Interstate Commerce Commission, and later its successor the Surface Transportation Board. The Class I mega-mergers happening around the same time drew much more attention and scrutiny. These purchases did, however, change the nature of competition within Wisconsin. The added lines allowed for more efficiencies for WC, yet sections of the state, particularly northeast Wisconsin, would have only one carrier and one route to the national network. Green Bay, for instance, had eight mainlines of four railroads serving the city on their own track in 1980. By 2000, three mainlines remained with WC offering the only connection to the wider national network (Escanaba & Lake Superior Railroad ran north into Michigan but only interchanged with WC). WC was well-run and a driver of growth in Wisconsin, but the network changes were permanent and would be with us much longer than the WC would be.

WC's modest fleet of switch engines tended to be found around the large yards at Fond du Lac and Stevens Point but would travel too. One of their more common outposts was the division point of Gladstone, MI. Gladstone warranted its own yard job both for blocking cars for the road trains as well as making the short trip to switch the large paper mill on the Escanaba River, a couple miles west of the yard. Here WC 1564 is backing down the mainline in front of train SOFD (Sault Ste. Marie–Fond du Lac) so it can clear up for train GBSO, which is about to arrive at Gladstone. February 6, 2000.

A shuttle train of aggregates bound for Illinois passes over the placid waters of the Fox River near Mukwonago, WI, near sunset as the moon rises in the east. L052 provides the sort of short haul service, less than 100 miles, that had been almost entirely turned over from large railroads to trucks by the 1980s. The WC recognized an opportunity to meet the demand for a shuttle train that would serve the Chicago area construction market using one crew per round trip. Short trips but the cars were moving another revenue load almost every day. May 30, 1996.

1

BEFORE WC:
Midwestern Railroad Formation, Competition, and Decline

To understand the factors that led to the creation of the new WC, we'll take a brief look at the history of railroading in the region.

RAILROAD CONSTRUCTION IN WISCONSIN

The earliest lines in Wisconsin were extensions of pioneering lines constructed north from Illinois as well as lines extending inland from Great Lakes ports, particularly Lake Michigan. Wisconsin's railway age began in the 1850s with extensions of the Chicago & North Western predecessors building into southeastern Wisconsin and companies that would later form the Milwaukee Road building a network of lines west from Milwaukee as far as the Mississippi River and into Iowa and Minnesota. Both companies kept building to establish their territories in the 1860s, generally from south to north and from east to west. Companies in places like Peshtigo built their own lines to reach inland from Lake Michigan. By the late 1860s, new companies that would comprise the Chicago, St. Paul, Minneapolis, and Omaha Railway Co. ("the Omaha") were building a network in the northwest part of the state.

The railroad building momentum continued in the 1870s, reaching new corners of the state. What would be the mainline of the Green Bay & Western started construction west from its namesake city in 1871 and, in three years, would reach all the way across the state to the Mississippi River. Also, in 1871, the original Wisconsin Central began construction with ambitions of connecting Lake Superior, central Wisconsin, and the cities on Lake Michigan by rail. Rugged terrain in the north was a persistent obstacle to construction, and it was not until 1877 that WC had a continuous route from the Fox Cities to Ashland.

By the 1880s, lumbering and mining had really taken off in northern Wisconsin and building continued with the Milwaukee, Lake Shore & Western reaching up from the Fox Cities to the border with Michigan to serve the newly opened Gogebic Iron Range. The Minneapolis,

Despite a lot of connections between carriers all over the Midwest, the Great Lakes are a natural barrier between the U.S. and Canada. The only link between Upper Michigan and Canada was at the far east end of the Soo Line and DSS&A where a series of bridges were constructed to span the St. Marys River and the Soo Locks. It would be the only international gateway for the Wisconsin Central. At the Soo, the railroad bridges to Ontario are right next to the I-75 bridge. WC 3000 is crossing the border with train OACTI (ore-Algoma Central-Tilden Mine) and will pause for customs clearance in the Soo Yard. This train shuttled iron ore pellets from the Marquette Range to the steel mill at Sault Ste. Marie, Ontario. The westbound trip consists of empty steel hopper cars and a couple cars of general freight right behind the power on September 30, 2001.

The Plymouth Sub had been a mainline for Milwaukee Road but was a quiet branch for WC. It was rare to see more than one train along here. The 2252 is on local L026; they have paused at Mequon to pick up the 4010 off a work train of ballast cars. A burp of cool exhaust emerges from the GP40M as it comes to life. After coupling the power together, these units will work to the south end of the subdivision then back north again this day. November 12, 1998.

St. Paul and Sault Ste. Marie built its route from the Twin Cities across northern Wisconsin to Upper Michigan and the Canadian border at Sault Ste. Marie. Like the others, it would move a lot of logs and lumber out of the Northwoods, but its initial backing and purpose was to ship the abundant flour produced at Minnesota mills to the east coast without encountering the middlemen of Chicago. The WC kept branching out from its original trunk yet it never did build into Milwaukee as planned, instead securing trackage rights over the Milwaukee Road from Rugby Jct. (near present-day Slinger) to Milwaukee. The same decade did see them build south from Slinger to Chicago, as well as extending west to the Twin Cities from Abbotsford. In the far north, Northern Pacific built east to Ashland and the Duluth, South Shore, and Atlantic was building its own line west towards the Twin Ports from Michigan. In the south, Illinois Central built north into Wisconsin reaching Madison and Dodgeville.

Plenty of construction was still happening in the 1890s and in the first decade of the twentieth century as all the companies built out their networks to secure more business. There were also plenty of financial moves with mature and stronger companies leasing other railroads when opportunities presented themselves. Much of the Wisconsin Central had been leased by the Northern Pacific in 1890, but the Panic of 1893 and following depression led to the end of the lease. Chicago & North Western had a controlling interest in the Omaha Road by 1882. In the early twentieth century, moves continued to be made, and by 1909, the Soo Line would commence a 999-year lease of the Wisconsin Central. Thus, by the 1910s, the bulk of the railroad construction was complete in Wisconsin and the three players were stratified into Soo Line (including WC), C&NW (including C. M. St.P. & O.) and the Milwaukee Road who crisscrossed the state reaching nearly every major city. This status quo would hold for nearly seventy years.

It is worth acknowledging the presence of another Class I railroad with a long presence in the state: the Chicago, Burlington & Quincy (later Burlington Northern, today BNSF Railway). Their line running the length of the Mississippi shoreline of Wisconsin has long been a heavy traffic corridor, but for the purposes of this synopsis somewhat separate from the impacts that shaped railroading in the rest of the state.

EARLY TWENTIETH-CENTURY REFINEMENTS

Once the three statewide railroads were established, they set about improving and investing in their properties to stay competitive. The C&NW made a major investment in building the "Adams Cutoff." A line of almost entirely new construction that angled away from Milwaukee through Adams in central Wisconsin to a junction with the Omaha Road subsidiary at Wyeville on the existing Chicago–Twin Cities mainline. The Adams route was built to a high standard with generous cuts and fills featuring plenty of grade-separated road crossings. Built to expedite freight and passengers, it passed though sparsely populated countryside.

The Milwaukee Road also made investments in its mainline across Wisconsin. All three companies had continued to build out their networks to the west across Minnesota and the Dakotas, and the new lines pulled in more traffic that would find its way across Wisconsin. In the case of the Milwaukee Road, they built all the way to the west coast via Montana, Idaho, and Washington. With all the midwestern and western traffic travelling the Milwaukee mainline, it was built up into a well-maintained double-track speedway across the state. The C&NW would be double tracked across much of its core route as well. While the Soo Line was also busy in these decades, it did not build double track outside of some short stretches in and near the biggest cities they served. The Milwaukee and the C&NW were in speed races against the CB&Q and each other for Chicago–Twin Cities passenger travel. The Soo Line was never able to compete in this corridor due to the extra miles their route covered. Rather than high speed from city to city, the Soo trains were heavy with mail and its passengers were more likely to be destined for one of the cities or resorts of central Wisconsin.

Despite the single track of the Soo Line, there was still plenty of investment in their mainlines while others were burnishing theirs. Around the time of the Soo Line–WC lease, a new line was put in branching off their Twin Cities line at Owen up to Superior providing another outlet for freight moving between the northland and Chicago. Right on the heels of the lease, work began on numerous improvements to the line from Chippewa Falls into Minnesota. Three large segments of track were bypassed with brand-new alignments greatly reducing the grades and curvature. The showpiece of this work was the steel-arch Arcola High Bridge crossing the St. Croix River from blufftop to blufftop. It is worth noting that from early on in Soo Line history, Canadian Pacific had a majority stake and controlling interest. With connections at Portal, ND, in the west and Sault Ste. Marie, MI, in the east, the Soo Line was a natural extension of CP's interests.

Some railroad improvements of the early twentieth century were truly monumental in scale. Perhaps the grandest landmark on the new Wisconsin Central is found where the line crosses from Wisconsin to Minnesota. High above the St. Croix River, the Arcola High Bridge crosses from blufftop to blufftop on five steel arches. It replaced a much lower bridge and miles of steep grades and sharp curves that led down into the valley, across the river, and back up the other side. On September 21, 1997, WC 6588 leads an empty coke train west into Minnesota.

MID-CENTURY CHANGES

After the roaring '20s, the Great Depression hit all the railroads hard, with traffic plummeting and marginal branch lines starting to be abandoned. More specific to Wisconsin and Upper Michigan, industries were starting to mature, transition, and consolidate. An early source of traffic in the northern part of the state was based on logging the vast forests and shipping finished lumber to customers around the country. Once the large pines of the virgin forests were exhausted, large timber companies such as Weyerhaeuser moved on to the Pacific Northwest. Some of the cut-over lands were cleared for new farms, although the soil and climate prevented widescale agricultural success beyond pockets of hardy crops such as potatoes or hay to support small dairies. More common across the north was natural regeneration of the forest, often with faster growing "volunteer" species such as aspen. Of course, the wood produced by these young forests would need decades of growth to produce even a fraction of the lumber old growth provided. Instead, many of the sawmill cities pivoted to a new industry: papermaking. The railroads reached all corners of the Northwoods and papermills would be built where the abundant sources of waterpower were previously used for sawmills. Pulpwood was the new staple of traffic for these northern routes.

Even though the pulpwood traffic was steady, changes to the network continued. The smaller logs along with advances in truck capacity and improvements in the highway network contributed to a steady pruning of the dead-end logging branches into the woods. At the mill end of the operations, the network was a benefit to industry as most companies were served by multiple railroads. Some built-up areas, such as Wisconsin Rapids, were served by all three major carriers plus the Green Bay & Western. So much competition was good for the shippers but kept the margins on all this traffic slim for the carriers. The low-priority (slow-moving) traffic and deferred maintenance took its toll on these secondary lines over the ensuing years of the mid-twentieth century. Financial trouble on the C&NW and the Milwaukee left their routes in tough shape with a steady cadence of abandonment filings by the 1960s and 1970s. Soo Line had long taken a more cautious and conservative approach to running their railroad and maintained a strong presence across the northland during this period. The 1961 merger with the Wisconsin Central and the Duluth, South Shore and Atlantic cemented the previous coordination through lease between the SOO and WC, while the DSS&A combination made SOO the dominant railroad in Upper Michigan reaching most corners of that territory.

END GAME

By 1977, the Milwaukee Road had been losing $100 million a year and was in receivership, multiple plans and proposals were in the works to save as much of the railroad as possible. The scheme ultimately selected for post-bankruptcy was christened "Milwaukee II." Milwaukee II saw the abandonment of the Milwaukee transcontinental route from Miles City, MT, to Puget Sound along with line sales and abandonments across the Midwest. Several hundred miles of branch lines across southern Wisconsin would be purchased by the state. In northern Wisconsin, the old Superior Division from Green Bay north to Ontonagon, MI, was spun off to the Escanaba & Lake Superior Railroad. The much smaller Milwaukee Road was profitable,

There was plenty of well-kept mainline included in the WC sale. A nice example of this infrastructure is the bridge over the Escanaba River just downstream from the Mead papermill, a major WC customer in Upper Michigan. A borrowed DM&IR locomotive heads up a westbound local for Hermansville, MI, and Pembine, WI. August 18, 1996.

Around the new WC were a lot of facilities from an earlier era. On the shore of Lake Superior, Marquette, MI, had been the headquarters of predecessor Duluth, South Shore & Atlantic. It had been several decades since a roundhouse of this size had been needed, but WC made good use of the offices and a few stalls. Nearby, a large ore dock, silent since the early 1970s, dominates the Marquette waterfront. December 26, 1996.

With plenty of lightly constructed branches employing worn-out first-generation diesels, the Milwaukee Road of the late 1960s was looking for new power with light axle loading for their branches. Ten SDL39 locomotives were built by EMD in two orders for Milwaukee Road. Only nine made it to the Soo Line after one was wrecked (581) and none wore full SOO colors before all nine were sold to WC when the railroad was created. The SDL39s were well-suited to serving branches around northern Wisconsin and Upper Michigan but could turn up anywhere on the WC. On May 27, 1994, a pair of the 2,300-hp units run alongside Keweenaw Bay at Baraga, MI.

but its reduced size made it into an attractive takeover target for neighboring railroads. The Grand Trunk Western offered to take on the Milwaukee Road debt in exchange for the assets of the railroad. In response, C&NW and Soo Line made offers to purchase the Milwaukee Road. In a long-running bidding war, C&NW and SOO repeatedly upped their offers until the judge overseeing the bankruptcy reorganization selected the SOO offer as being in the public interest, despite being a lower cash bid. The ramifications of this merger would echo through the rest of the decade and lead to the creation of the Wisconsin Central.

The Soo Line had its work cut out for it in taking on a railroad that had suffered years of differed maintenance. Each company had their own culture and way of doing things built up over a century. There was also an over-abundance of trackage across Wisconsin and Minnesota that needed a fresh look to determine what the best operating plan was going to be. Despite the well-maintained SOO mainline between Chicago and the Twin Cities, it was longer than the Milwaukee Road mainline and did not have the capacity to handle the traffic of both carriers. So once the combination was complete, Soo Line moved all through traffic to the Milwaukee Road and started work on repairing and modernizing that corridor. As a condition of the Milwaukee Road sale, the ICC stipulated that the SOO divest itself of lines to preserve competition. SOO would set up the "Lake States Transportation Division" comprised mostly of the old SOO routes east of Minneapolis and lines such as the old Milwaukee Road Valley Division through Wisconsin Rapids and Wausau up to Tomahawk. The hope was for Lake States to focus on customers on these now secondary lines and try to establish flexible work rules for the crews running the trains. When the gains attempted by the new division were hard to come by, SOO started abandonment proceedings for the marginal lines, then considered selling off Lake States altogether. This would raise money and allow the SOO to focus on their efforts on modernizing and integrating the remaining SOO-MILW property.

By creating Lake States, Soo Line had defined what was to be available for purchase as a new regional railroad stretching between Chicago and Superior, WI, Minneapolis and Sault Ste. Marie, MI. SOO had in large measure also split its locomotive fleet, with a lot of the older well-worn twenty- to thirty-year-old locomotives pulling the Lake States trains. The crews, however, were still represented by the various operating unions and held seniority across the SOO-MILW system. There were some employees who would stay on after the sale with the new carrier, but the vast majority would use their seniority to "bump" into jobs at various other SOO terminals around the Midwest once the sale was consummated. The Lake States Division was put up for sale in January 1987, and in April, it was announced that a new company, "Wisconsin Central Ltd.," had reached an agreement to purchase the property from Soo Line pending ICC approval.

Opposite page:

Above: Mergers of the 1970s and 1980s shook up the railroad scene around the country. The upper Midwest was no exception. Before 1985, Shoreham Hill was a double-tracked section of the SOO mainline from Minneapolis to Chicago. After the Milwaukee Road merger, SOO traffic from the west got on the BN via trackage rights to access the former Milwaukee Road mainline at St. Paul. Once that happened, the old SOO up the hill was very quiet. One track was removed and the only manifest train through here in the WC-era was the daily train to Stevens Point, seen here passing over the switch at Central Ave. The grade of the removed second main can be seen to the left of the WC transfer, led by an ex-BN SD45. November 11, 1992.

Below: Despite the name, the Duluth, South Shore & Atlantic only had a few stretches where the mainline directly traced the south shore of Lake Superior. From Harvey, MI, curving into Marquette from the east along Marquette Bay, the mainline hugged the shore with only a handful of feet between the ends of the ties and the waves. Jordan spreader 315 was originally C&NW property that went with the Fox River Valley sale and onto the WC roster when Fox Valley & Western took over. The 315 sure came in handy this day clearing the mainline, Marquette's lower yard and the track up the hill to Negaunee. In about a month, WC would purchase Union Pacific's tracks north of Green Bay and this route would fall silent. December 29, 1996.

The large hulking wooden station at Gladstone, MI, speaks to its importance as a division point along the original Soo Line mainline between Minneapolis and Sault Ste. Marie, MI. In addition to division offices, Gladstone once boasted a large grain elevator on the shore of Little Bay de Noc to serve ships on Lake Michigan, it was the first lakehead reached by the old Soo headed east. There is still an active large yard here and a portion of the roundhouse (rebuilt after a tornado) to service power between assignments. Once the ex-C&NW properties were purchased in the area, WC had plenty of offices and the old station here was replaced with a single level modular yard office. June 15, 1993.

After the turbulent 1960s, the future of railroading was decidedly murky, like this view from a caboose cupola at North Ironwood, MI. One of advantages WC presented was the reduction of train crew sizes by at least half and the elimination of cabooses on most runs. The plot twist here is the presence of the caboose on this train was part of an effort to reduce the crew size to one for certain assignments. The ex-Algoma Central caboose has been outfitted with all the gear necessary to enable any locomotive to couple to the caboose and be run remotely from the ground. May 10, 1996.

2

WC STARTUP:
Early Operations, New Traffic Patterns, Carload Recovery, and Growth

From a bumpy day one it didn't take long for the new railroad to start bringing back some customers that had turned their backs on shipping by rail years before.

A NEW DAY AND AN OLD NAME

In the buildup to the ICC approval and closing of the deal, management of the WC made preparations for launching the new operation, lining up employees, and securing second-hand locomotives to power the trains. Most notably, WC picked up a fleet of ex-Burlington Northern SD45s. September 11, 1987 was to be the day the sale would close. An eleventh-hour decision by the ICC put the sale on hold for up to forty-five days. Rather than let their locomotive assets languish, WC leased the SD45s to other carriers on a short-term basis. Instead of taking the forty-five days, the ICC greenlighted the sale in less than a month. This meant the scramble was on to gear up for day one. The SD45s would not be done with their leases yet, so power from other sources was utilized to bridge the gap until WC's six-axle power came home. Some of these interim units were older power that Soo Line had assigned to the Lake States territory. Lake States had become a bastion of old first- and second-generation Soo Line power. Some of these, such as the GP30s and most of the GP35s, would be part of the sale to Wisconsin Central. Even older power, GP7s and GP9s, would be leased by WC for a time to keep things rolling but would ultimately go home to the Soo Line once the power crunch eased.

When October 11, 1987 dawned, the new railroad was born. The locomotive struggles were just the beginning as a problem with the car accounting computers made for a transition that resulted in all the car data being lost. All the cars on the new railroad were unknown on day one. Employees had to manually comb through every siding, yard, and customer spur to determine what cars were on the new system.

Most of the railroaders on the new WC came from other railroads and other careers seeking new opportunities and new adventures. The new railroad was non-union so more flexibility, more opportunity but also some risk was inherent for those who signed on with the upstart. WC management counted on lower operating costs from the beginning. The agreements Lake States/SOO was operating under still required a caboose on road trains along with larger crews. From the beginning, WC road trains would have a two-person crew and no caboose. Crews were encouraged to reach out to current and past shippers to win back traffic that may have been neglected in recent years. There was an undeniable energy among this newly formed family of railroaders who choose to either stay on for the change from SOO to WC or join from around the country (or farther) and use that personal stake to help make the WC a success.

MAKING SENSE OF THE NEW OPERATION ON OLD TRACKS

There were changes to the traditional routes that made up this territory starting in the Lake States period. SOO had found itself with some parallel routes once the Milwaukee Road sale was completed, and a new focus overall. Places such as central Wisconsin had seen new routings in use that continued with the new WC. A prime example was the Ashland Sub and the Valley Sub. From the construction of the first original Wisconsin Central mainline and for well over 100 years through the purchase of the Milwaukee Road, traffic flowed from Ashland south to Spencer. When the Valley Sub joined the fold with the rest of the Milwaukee Road, SOO had two north–south lines in central Wisconsin. When scrutinized against each other, the south end of the Ashland Sub was found to have a scattering of small shippers when compared to the large paper mills (and a power plant) that dotted the length of the parallel section of the Valley Sub. Even though the north end of the Valley Sub no longer crossed the SOO tracks at Heafford Jct., the Tomahawk Railway connected the two between Tomahawk and Bradley. By rerouting Ashland-bound trains over the Valley Sub and the Tomahawk Railway to Lake States tracks, the Ashland Sub between Medford and Prentice was able to be taken out of service. A local would serve the remaining customers on what was now the Medford Sub, and the rails of the unused portion would be lifted early in the WC's tenure.

It did not take too much imagination to conjure up who was the previous owner of either the railroad or the locomotives in the early days of the new Wisconsin Central. Such is the case with this local hustling east at Sheridan, WI. The worn paint on this GP30 is classic Soo Line and the route was the backbone of the SOO across central Wisconsin until the mid-1980s. April 29, 1998.

The relationship of the WC to the Tomahawk Railway is evident in the makeup of this train headed to the large PCA mill on the TR. The WC trains to the Bradley Sub also used this combination wood and steel bridge over the Wisconsin River. The Milwaukee Road bridge, just to the east of this crossing, was abandoned and is now part of the Hiawatha Trail. March 12, 2005.

Opposite page:

Above: After delivering their inbound cars for the Burlington Northern at Northtown Yard in Minneapolis, the WC transfer is in the T-Yard with the pickup of their outbound cars. From here they will diverge into Soo Line's Shoreham Yard and climb Shoreham Hill to New Brighton and the Minnesota Commercial interchange, ultimately reaching WC rails at Withrow, MN, east of the Twin Cities. SD45s wearing BN green and Geeps in SOO red and white (light grey) were a common sight in the early years of the WC. November 11, 1992.

Below: The WC had plenty of humble outposts around the system including this office at Ashland, WI. There was not usually a need for large offices, just a place for a telephone, FAX machine, and a couple cases of water. Section gangs could report for duty here and train crews could receive updated train lists. The Ashland office felt extra-humble situated about a block from the grand passenger station built of sandstone which was repurposed as a brewery and restaurant by this time. January 16, 1993.

WC 6498 wears the first version of the Wisconsin Central paint scheme, featuring chevron stripes on the nose. This pair of SD45s strain against a train of iron ore from the Minnesota Iron Range. Destined for an Indiana steel mill, this train is approaching the crest of Byron Hill, south of Fond du Lac. March 23, 1996.

The railroad car ferry to lower Michigan, along with the line to St. Ignace that served it, was no longer in operation by the time the WC was formed. A stub of the old line had been retained at Trout Lake as a popular place for Soo Line to meet opposing road trains. It was also used by Marquette-bound trains into the WC era. This L043 has built its outbound train in the yard (to the left of the depot) and backed around the connection track. Momentarily it will make an early morning departure across the diamond with the SOO Sub and back to Marquette via Newberry. July 17, 1991.

A former Soo Line GP35 leads train L088 south (railroad east) down the Valley Sub approaching Junction City. Part of the WC's approach to winning back traffic was to run shorter, more frequent trains between customers and smaller yards such as Wausau and larger hubs like Stevens Point. March 16, 1996.

A less common early variant of the WC paint scheme Is seen on this SD45 at Gladstone, MI. The V-stripe was seen on plenty of units, but this variation features a mini-logo on the nose. Other versions had a large logo placed on top of the upper stripe while others ran without a nose logo. August 13, 1992.

There were other such stretches that were idle when WC came into existence that did not get a reprieve from abandonment, such as a stretch of the original SOO mainline between Amery and Almena in western Wisconsin. Once home to a daily road freight between Minneapolis and Sault Ste. Marie into the mid-1980s, it became idle with no through traffic and no local customers.

As was often the case when regionals were carved out of existing railroads, the selling railroads took steps designed to have the new regional carrier gather and feed traffic to the existing railroad without allowing freedom to solicit competing through traffic and undercut the legacy carrier. Soo Line had moved the eastern Canada-midwestern U.S.-western Canada traffic to a routing across lower Michigan and kept that arrangement with parent Canadian Pacific after selling the Lake States Division. They also did not sell all the track to Minneapolis nor enough track to make independent connections with other railroads in Minnesota. SOO only sold track to WC as far as Withrow, MN, the point where the lines from Sault Ste. Marie and Chicago came together just a handful of miles into Minnesota. Per the new railroads' operating plan, traffic from all over the western part of the railroad would be marshalled at the Stevens Point yard on the Twin Cities–Chicago mainline. Thus, it would be the only through route to the west. The western remnant of the Minneapolis–Sault Ste. Marie route would be served by a local based out of New Brighton, MN (on CP tracks reached via trackage rights), with the rails removed east of Amery.

Among the changes that came about in the wake of the Soo Line takeover of the Milwaukee Road was a "new" connection between Milwaukee's Valley line and the original SOO mainline via the Tomahawk Railway. SOO Lake States acquired trackage rights over the Tomahawk Railway from Tomahawk on the ex-MILW to Bradley on the SOO. This carried over to the new WC operation. After a few years and with the WC interchanging with the Tomahawk Railway at Tomahawk and Jersey City, WC purchased the track up to Bradley. L012 is seen on the ex-Tomahawk track at Jersey City, just north of Tomahawk. The Tomahawk Railway heritage is hinted at by the unique milepost "B 2" (2 miles from Bradley) seen to the right of the locomotive. October 3, 1998.

The morning sun shines on the flank of a WC Russell snowplow on a stub track at Gladstone, MI. This piece of venerable equipment spent many years on the Soo Line. With a fresh coat of WC paint, it is still an essential piece of rolling stock for keeping the lines open. It is silently waiting for the inevitability of another tough midwestern winter when it is needed again. September 6, 1998.

At North Escanaba, the Escanaba & Lake Superior ducks under the WC Pembine Sub. The stacks of the Mead paper mill can be seen in the distance. The WC made service to the paper industry a priority by thoroughly testing their paper service boxcars against water leaks. A tiny leak in the roof could damage the large rolls of paper inside, resulting in a rejected load at a customer's dock. WC promoted this relationship as evidenced by the sign on the overpass "Wisconsin Central, a Mead partner in customer satisfaction." August 13, 1992.

It was not just locomotives that were painted up to promote the railroad, even school busses could be found sporting the maroon and gold. This bus is parked in Norway, MI, between assignments. The bus was used to shuttle maintenance of way gangs between their worksites and lodging during large track projects around the system. September 7, 1998.

Snow drifts and icicles hang from the depot at L'Anse, MI. The station was once a stop for the *Copper Country Limited* that ran from Chicago to Calumet, MI, but was mostly empty by this time, housing a FAX machine and some maintenance of way tools. It would be razed a few years later. A pair of DM&IR SD9s power train L041 this day as they depart for the trip up L'Anse Hill on the way back to Marquette. December 26, 1995.

At the northwest corner of Wisconsin, WC 6548 on a transfer to the BN returns to South Itasca via the Saunders connection from BN to the Duluth, Missabe & Iron Range Interstate Branch. At the same time, a long transfer from the Duluth, Winnipeg & Pacific Pokegama Yard is also returning behind WC 6594, passing under the BN on the Interstate Branch. August 25, 1993.

While all of WC's tracks were east of the Mississippi River, they did cross the big river to interchange with CP Rail at Humboldt Yard in northwest Minneapolis. GP40 3004 and a GP35 have their outbound cars in hand as they begin the trip back east. October 17, 1992.

Several lightly trafficked lines were being considered by Soo Line for abandonment by the mid-1980s, including much of the remaining DSS&A routes. Rather than abandon lines such as the L'Anse Sub, WC sought new/revived traffic while providing regular service to the existing traffic base. WC 584 hustles east across the Peshekee River near where it empties into Lake Michigamme west of Champion, MI, with a handful of cars from L'Anse. June 21, 1993.

Dubbed the "White Pine Flyer" by some, L045 made slow but steady progress on three trips per week to serve the White Pine Mine. Even after mining stopped at White Pine copper continued to arrive by rail for refining, this provided boxcar loads in both directions. WC 3003 has just traversed the 14-mile branch south from the mine and is back on the old DSS&A mainline, passing the depot at Bergland, MI. May 17, 1997.

Seen here at Van Dyne, WI, there were a handful of these Magnetic Flagman-style "wig-wag" crossing signals still in service on ex-Soo Line routes when the WC was formed. Dating back to the 1940s and earlier, they stayed in place until replaced by newer signals when they either failed or were upgraded. March 23, 1996.

T205, WC 7554 west, is crossing the old "Skally Line" at Bald Eagle, MN. The WC is operating on CP Rail track at this point. The automated crossing here includes smashboard mechanisms, although the smashboards themselves are removed from along the CP track. The signals on the old Northern Pacific track show the smashboards positioned against what is now a Minnesota Commercial industrial branch. Smashboards are a rather old, but effective, method of establishing fault when a train disregards a stop signal. Once the board has been smashed by the train it provides proof positive of who passed a red signal. May 9, 1998.

Right: Looking north on the "Skally Line" the smashboard is positioned to foul the ex-Northern Pacific main track. When this automatic crossing is ready to allow northbound traffic, a clear signal will display and the smashboard will pivot to the vertical position. May 9, 1998.

Below: While not obvious at first glance, the single track mainline of the Chicago Sub was the busiest corridor on the WC system. Acting as a funnel for traffic from all over northern Wisconsin and beyond, destined to the various connections around the nation's railroad hub. This winter morning view was taken just south of Allenton, WI, looking south. December 7, 1996.

3

EARLY TWEAKS TO THE WISCONSIN CENTRAL SYSTEM

Changes to what had been Soo Line's Lake States Division not only began with a jolt on October 11, 1987 but continued through the early years as the railroad was in a constant state of evolution.

PICKING UP THE MUNISING BRANCH

In Upper Michigan, the iron ore-hauling short-line Lake Superior & Ishpeming maintained a remnant of their once-extensive network to serve the Kimberly-Clark paper mill at Munising, MI. Isolated from the rest of the LS&I, the Munising branch's sole connection to the outside world was via the WC Newberry Sub at Munising Jct., 5.49 miles south of Munising. Since 1979 when their own track between Marquette and Munising Jct. was abandoned, LS&I stationed one of their ALCO RS-3s on the branch and taxied a crew from Marquette to Munising to switch the mill and interchange as needed. After ten years of operating this isolated trackage, the LS&I elected to sell the branch. By this time, the rest of the LS&I ALCO locomotive fleet had been retired and they had moved to a standardized roster consisting solely of ex-Burlington Northern, General Electric U30Cs.

WC was the most logical suitor for the Munising operations and took over the branch in 1989 as its "Munising Spur." The tracks between Munising Jct. and Munising had not seen much investment in the later years of the LS&I, and it was FRA excepted track restricted to 10 mph for quite some time until the WC could stabilize the track. It would later be upgraded to a 20-mph maximum speed. Subsequent abandonments in the 1990s would see the old DSS&A mainline cut at Munising Jct. and abandoned from there west to beyond Marquette. Munising would continue to be served from the east. Interestingly, due to the track arrangement at Munising Jct., the train would still traverse a switchback and run around the cars in each direction both to and from Munising since the two lines connected via a southeast quadrant connection with an overpass where the old DSS&A mainline passed over the one-time Munising Railroad. While not providing a flood of traffic, the Munising business would be a steady contributor to tonnage coming off the old DSS&A at Trout Lake for the rest of the WC's time.

Most of the time, the Munising branch was switched by the road trains on their way from Marquette to Trout Lake. End cab switchers were extremely rare on the old DSS&A or the Munising branch so finding the WC 1235 switching near the mill was quite a surprise. South Bay of Lake Superior can be seen in the distance. August 11, 1993.

LS&I RS3 1604 had been stationed at Munising in the late 1980s to switch the paper mill and make the run up to the WC interchange at Munising Jct. Once that isolated operation was sold off, it returned to Eagle Mills until sold to the Wisconsin & Michigan where it served as their second locomotive. Unfortunately, Wisconsin & Michigan would be at odds with WC within just three years and the lease would be terminated with the equipment gathered up and shipped out. 1604 is seen at Ironwood on January 16, 1993.

SELLING THE NESTORIA-SIDNAW SEGMENT

Farther west along the old DSS&A some routing options were explored as WC served the White Pine Mine on a 14-mile-long branch extending north from Bergland, MI. The line between Nestoria and Bergland (Sidnaw Sub) was largely out of service, but some test trains were run to serve the mine from the direction of Marquette. Ultimately, White Pine Mine would be served out of the west via the Marengo Jct. connection to the Ashland Sub. Lacking any other customers or through traffic, the Sidnaw Sub from Sidnaw to Bergland would be abandoned and removed. Sidnaw was a connection with the Escanaba & Lake Superior Railroad (ex-Milwaukee Road line to Ontonagon, MI). WC did bring one special into Sidnaw over this line, the *Northwoods Explorer* private car excursion in July 1990. The varnish was handed off here to the E&LS for the rare miles trip over their line to Ontonagon, MI.

Around this time, there was a group in northern Houghton County studying the possibility of attracting a new operator to reopen the old Soo Line tracks through Chassell and Houghton, dormant since 1982. The tracks north of the county line were state owned. E&LS was a leading candidate to operate the segment. To reach the northern Houghton County track, E&LS purchased the Sidnaw to Nestoria segment from WC and procured trackage rights over WC from Nestoria to Arnheim where they would reach the state-owned segment.

Ultimately, the resumption of service to Houghton over this route would not come to pass. E&LS would, however, use the line to Nestoria in 1993 for a short-lived interchange of log cars, loaded at L'Anse on the WC, handed off to E&LS at Nestoria, then hauled by them to a mill in

Once WC decided there were no prospects along the Sidnaw Sub, the tracks from Sidnaw to Bergland were abandoned and removed. The tracks form Sidnaw to Nestoria were sold to the Escanaba & Lake Superior who connected at Sidnaw. There was also an effort by E&LS to serve northern Houghton County via trackage rights over the WC. Although the trains to Houghton would not come to pass, E&LS and WC did interchange log traffic at Nestoria for a time. This routing shaved many miles off the trip to Quinnesec, but having three railroads handle the cars kept the margins too low and this traffic did not last long. WC and E&LS trains converge at Nestoria on July 27, 1993 to swap loaded wood rack cars for empties.

the Iron Mountain area (on the C&NW). The cost of having multiple carriers handle the loads meant the E&LS did not make money on the moves and they were short-lived. After that, the Nestoria line would largely remain silent until years later when the business of storing surplus railcars boomed and E&LS would store miles of cars on the old DSS&A mainline.

LEASING THE BESSEMER BRANCH

At the far west end of the Upper Peninsula, the SOO's Bessemer Sub had at one time been a heavy source of iron ore tonnage off the Gogebic Iron Range brought west into Wisconsin then north from Mellen to the huge dock at Ashland. Iron mining on the Gogebic Iron Range wound down sooner than it did on the other Michigan ranges, with the last open mine closing in 1967. Other traffic that moved over the branch steadily declined into the 1980s with only occasional increases to supply special projects such as gas pipeline construction. Regular service was no longer provided at the time WC was formed. With a handful of small customers and heavy rail still in place from its days as a heavy ore route, WC entertained leasing this branch to a short-line operator. The Wisconsin & Michigan (WAND) started operations on the Bessemer branch in 1992, first with an ex-Calumet & Hecla 45-ton GE center-cab unit #211, soon joined by ex-LS&I RS-3 #1604, which had been rendered surplus when LS&I sold the Munising Spur to the WC.

The branch from Mellen, WI, to Bessemer, MI, was idle by the time WC took over the Lake States track and remained so in the early years. In 1992, Craig Burroughs leased this line from WC and started his Wisconsin & Michigan operation (like the WC, the second railroad by this name). Starting with an ex-Calumet & Hecla GE 45-tonner. Eventually, Wisconsin & Michigan would have a fleet of ex-Algoma Central cabooses and coaches, four ex-LS&I U23Cs among other equipment used on freight and passenger operations. On November 26, 1994, the 2301 rests at the Ironwood depot just 437 miles from Chicago via Mellen, Spencer and Fond du Lac.

After the Wisconsin & Michigan lease was terminated, WC honored the remaining pulpwood contract and made a few trips over the Bessemer branch to move that traffic. Among the last cars were these gondolas loaded on the main track at Upson, WI. For a time, WC had considered building a couple mile-long extension off the end of this line to connect with the White Pine Sub north of Bessemer. Such a connection would have allowed the WC to abandon the west end of the White Pine Sub, including the large trestles at Bad River and Vaughn Creek. Ultimately, the heavy rail dating to this line's time as a heavy iron ore hauling route was removed for reuse elsewhere. January 14, 1995.

It was a rare occurrence that WC leased a line to a short-line operator. Given their efficiencies and the aggressiveness with which they sought out new traffic and courted previously disgruntled customers, most shippers would be served by the WC itself. The 33.3-mile branch would need some brushing and potential shippers, a plywood plant, and a closed mine that shipped "paint ore" were at the far end. Undeterred, the WAND had big plans for the branch collecting a lot of old equipment, particularly a fleet of ex-LS&I GE U23Cs along with many streamlined coaches from the Algoma Central. With the passenger equipment, WAND started running a full slate of excursions out of their Ironwood depot. The branch hummed with activity for a few years, but by spring of 1995, WAND was at odds with the WC over lease payments. A long string of locomotives and cars were put together and moved off the branch to Mellen. From there, the collection would scatter to the four winds.

For a short time, WC would make an occasional run up part of the branch to honor a contract for hauling pulpwood that was still wrapping up when the WAND shut down. Despite consideration about possibly building a connection off the east end of the Bessemer branch north to connect with the old DSS&A to White Pine (this would allow WC to bypass the large Bad River Bridge on the old DSS&A), the tracks were removed from the Bessemer Sub once the last loads of pulpwood were hauled. The paint ore business that had been loaded in gondolas near the end of the branch was not lost; after abandonment, it was trucked to the siding at Thomaston on the White Pine Sub northeast of Bessemer. The Michigan portion of the Bessemer branch would be converted into the far west end of the statewide Iron-Belle Trail.

L039 travelling east on the original SOO mainline curves past Shepard Lake east of Rhinelander. A couple cars were picked up from the yard at Rhinelander, but the bulk of this train consists of gondola cars full of ore from the Flambeau Mine at Ladysmith destined for the smelters in Ontario. May 16, 1997.

Near the end of the Medford Sub sits this well-preserved depot. It is in private ownership and an interesting contrast to its sibling to the north at Park Falls. The Park Falls depot, still owned by the railroad, wore the Soo Line-applied "insulbrick" until the WC updated the exterior with vinyl siding. November 23, 1994.

The structures that came with the WC purchase ran the gamut, from modern to ruins. Defunct steam-era facilities such as the roundhouse at Park Falls had long outlived their usefulness, quietly awaiting a date with the wrecking ball as WC cleaned up obsolete corners of the property. June 1, 1994.

Three four-axle locomotives hustle train L012 south (timetable east) down the Valley Sub late on a winter's day at the tiny hamlet of Otis, WI. At one time, this line extended through Minocqua and Woodruff briefly serving lumber camps just beyond the state line into Upper Michigan. Although shortened, WC funneled a lot of traffic from the Northwoods down the Valley Sub. December 27, 1998.

One of the mainlines that did not fare well as a through route was the old Milwaukee Road Superior Division into Green Bay. Local customers on the Plymouth Sub were served via Hilbert and the Manitowoc Sub. Trackage rights over the GB&W was the preferred way for WC to reach Titletown, at least until the Fox River Valley purchase. Over time, the Plymouth Sub would be pruned back to Greenleaf and later Hilbert. Rails rust and weeds take over on the old Superior Division north of Hilbert, April 6, 1996.

WC Time Table No. 1 showed the L'Anse Sub intact all the way to the end of the track at Lake Linden. Despite the line last seeing freight service in 1982, there was hope for a revival to serve several industrial customers in the Keweenaw. These attempts faltered, but within *WC Time Table No. 3* (effective August 10, 1998), the L'Anse Sub included track as far as "New Chassell" 17.3 miles beyond the end of active track at Baraga. The WC intended to service a pulpwood landing developed at a closed drive-in theater adjacent to Highway 41. This too would not happen. A Pettibone speed swing was the only piece of WC equipment I would see on the rails past Baraga. I am not sure what work was being done, reportedly DSS&A had some unique track components that would sometimes be scrounged from unused sections. In time, Lake Superior would threaten to undercut Highway 41 here at Keweenaw Bay and the highway would be realigned onto the railroad right-of-way farther from the edge of the bluff. July 22, 1995.

The lower yard in Marquette followed along the lakefront south of downtown. WC 590 has just arrived from Trout Lake and performs some switching. After sorting out their cars, the crew will bring the power up to the roundhouse and go off duty. May 28, 1994.

A pair of SDL39s on train L042 switch the east end of Marquette's lower yard as they build their train for Trout Lake. At one time, there was an upper yard in Marquette up the hill from the ore dock to receive iron ore trains from the Marquette Range mines. The dock and upper yard were abandoned before the WC was started, leaving lower yard as WC's largest in the area. July 16, 1991.

To help move traffic efficiently to and from eastern connections, run-through power from those railroads was regularly seen on the Chicago Sub. T050 is led by one of Norfolk Southern's distinctive high-hood SD40-2s curving past the Burlington depot on May 4, 1996.

Marinette, Tomahawk & Western once had multiple lines radiating out from Tomahawk, WI. By the 1990s, successor Tomahawk Railway had a couple miles of track to serve a large mill at Wisconsin Dam, with all their traffic interchanging with Wisconsin Central. SW1500 1587 switches at Tomahawk, WI, on January 28, 2001.

Adding to the mix of traffic on the already busy Chicago Sub were trackage rights trains of the Wisconsin & Southern. From Rugby Jct. to Waukesha, trackage rights allowed WSOR to connect their northern and southern divisions. Train HJ (Horicon to Janesville) is seen approaching the switch at Grand Ave. in Waukesha where it will return to home rails. May 31, 1995.

With growing traffic, WC was in the market for more SD45s in 1994. The Santa Fe had some SD45s (and F45s, one FP45) on the market that WC picked up. Due to the ownership/lease details of these locomotives, WC had to lease them at the outset, they ran on the WC without renumbering or other changes for a time. On September 11, 1994, a pair of these locomotives are making up train T006 at New Brighton, MN.

One of WC's more remote junctions was found near the north end of the Ashland Sub at Marengo Jct. At one time, the Duluth, South Shore & Atlantic passed under the original Wisconsin Central here on its way to Duluth. Since 1935, it has been a junction where the DSS&A and later Soo Line connected to the Ashland mainline. For the WC, it was the west end of the White Pine Sub where cars were handed off. Early on, the White Pine trains would terminate at Mellen, later practice was to operate the White Pine train as a turn starting at North Ironwood and ultimately North Bessemer, swapping cars with the Ashland train at Marengo Jct. On October 3, 2001, a train was staged on the north leg of the wye to head to White Pine while WC 587 headed past with L1516, the Ashland turn on its way back to Mellen.

WC had a few customers along the shoreline in Ashland including the Fort James paper mill on the east edge of town. Time had just about run out for the long-standing shipper on November 24, 1997, as the Ashland turn retrieves a single boxcar. In time, all the customers along waterfront from the Reiss coal dock to the paper mill would cease to be active shippers.

L052, the southbound "rock job," cuts through Waukesha, WI, on the way to northern Illinois. With a solo SD45, the train runs in "hammerhead" formation on the way down. The searchlight signals protected the crossing of the C&NW at Grand Ave., which by this time was a connection to Union Pacific to the right (east) and a connection to the Wisconsin & Southern to the left (west) with the diamond crossing removed. September 22, 1996.

There was a lot of company pride in just about everything WC did. For instance, this signal relay cabinet saw new use as a shed at the layover point of North Bessemer, MI, on the White Pine Sub, but not before being dressed up in company colors complete with logo. December 28, 1997.

4

WC ACQUIRES C&NW ROUTE FROM CAMERON, WI, TO SOUTH ITASCA, WI

For roughly 20 years the Chicago & North Western had been steadily retrenching from its one-time expansive presence in northern Wisconsin. By the 1990s it had one primary route left across northwestern Wisconsin and one interested buyer.

AN OLD OMAHA MAINLINE

There was a time when a couple of mainlines in northwestern Wisconsin were known as the "great Omaha X" due to their appearance of symmetry on the state map. Constructed first was the North Wisconsin Railroad from Hudson, WI, to Bayfield, WI, on Lake Superior, later becoming part of the Chicago, Minneapolis, St. Paul & Omaha. The "Omaha Road" constructed a line between Eau Claire, WI, and Duluth, MN (completing the "X," which crossed the first line at Spooner–Trego, WI). The Omaha Road was controlled by the C&NW for most of its history and completely absorbed in 1972. The older portion of the "X" was largely abandoned in the 1980s as through traffic and local customers dwindled. The Eau Claire–Twin Ports line did stay active with through trains. Even though C&NW did not reach beyond Duluth, they did interchange with several railroads and garnered a share of southbound CN traffic off the Duluth, Winnipeg & Pacific headed to Chicago. By the 1990s, C&NW had refocused on handling a booming coal business out of Wyoming and the CN had reached a haulage arrangement with BN to handle whole trains of CN traffic between Superior, WI, and Chicago.

A SURPRISING SALE

It would seem the line to Itasca Yard (Superior, WI) was slowly headed for the same grim fate as the rest of the "Omaha X" and many other lines C&NW used to operate in northern Wisconsin. That is until news broke that Wisconsin Central Ltd. had reached a deal to purchase much of the route, from Cameron, WI (where it connected with WC's Barron Sub), to South Itasca, WI

(where it connected with the DM&IR Interstate Branch providing interchange access to the other carriers in the Twin Ports).

The WC and C&NW had teamed up to ship ore from the Minnesota Iron Range to the docks at Escanaba via the Cameron connection in the winter, but otherwise it was a surprise to hear of the sale. At first it was a little hard to make sense of the move. The SOO route WC already used from Ladysmith to Superior was in better condition than the C&NW route, and the old mainline between Cameron and Ladysmith would need a ton of work to host heavy traffic at reasonable speeds.

AN ACE IN THE HOLE

To understand the genius of this move, you had to look back at the terms of the sale that created the WC. The Soo Line did not want the WC competing for overhead traffic between the Twin Ports and Chicago. Like the Twin Cities–Chicago traffic, this was a market Soo Line would still be in. Despite abandoning all their own routes into Superior, the Soo Line would continue to serve the Twin Ports via trackage rights that Milwaukee Road had used over the BN for many years. The Wisconsin Central sale did not include the tracks from Superior to Ladysmith, WC,

L064 sails through Solon Springs over the ex-C&NW portion of the Superior Sub. The manicured right of way shows the steadily increasing importance of this line to WC for both their own and overhead traffic. WC 7520 was a commemorative unit denoting at least two of the railroads' anniversaries on the long hood and special lettering on the front and rear. June 3, 2000.

Just north of the new connection at Hayward Jct., the Superior Sub crosses the Namekagon River on this Pratt deck truss bridge, a shorter and lower version of the bridge this train will cross ahead (after dark) at Ladysmith. Low evening light above a nationally designated wild and scenic river is a great settling to feature a couple SD45s hauling tonnage across the northwoods. August 26, 1995.

was the sole operator on these tracks, but dispatching was done by the SOO between Weirgor (17 miles north of Ladysmith) and Stinson Yard.

Soo Line had no incentive to ease the lock they had on WC bridge traffic. For WC, the C&NW Itasca line provided a way out. As soon as they reached a deal with the C&NW, the hold Soo Line had was broken. The reason for the Soo Line to hold the northern Superior Sub was gone as well, SOO quickly sold the track to the WC. The WC would not need to rehab the Barron Sub or make the circuitous connection at Cameron, the biggest reason to purchase this track was as a giant bargaining chip and it worked. The WC now had two routes to Superior. Rather than choose one the WC took a "best of both" approach. The hill out of the Lake Superior Basin was a steeper climb on the ex-SOO route so the new Superior Sub would start out at South Itasca and take the ex-C&NW out of the basin and as far as Gordon, WI. At Gordon, the two lines had crossed at a grade-separated fly-over and a new connection was built here to allow trains to seamlessly pass off the ex-C&NW onto the ex-SOO for the remainder of their journey. To the north, the ex-SOO was abandoned all the way to Ambridge (with parts of an expanded US 53 built on top of the grade) and to the south the ex-C&NW was abandoned as far as Trego (and from Spooner to Rice Lake).

Despite being isolated from the rest of the Union Pacific system, UP did a steady business at Wisconsin Rapids. Their presence traces back to when predecessor C&NW had a route between Fond du Lac and Marshfield that passed through here. In addition to a local serving Wisconsin Rapids out of Adams (via trackage rights on WC from Necedah to Wisconsin Rapids) UP road trains to and from Itasca (Superior, WI) ran through here to Junction City where they would access the Superior Sub for the remainder of the trip north. The PRIT and ITPR trains started using this route after C&NW sold their own route between Cameron, WI, and Itasca to WC in 1992. On April 19, 1998, train MPRIT is passing WC L010 at Wisconsin Rapids Yard.

A trio of SD40-2s lead UP train PRITA over the Summit Creek trestle on the Superior Sub. Soo Line built a branch to Reserve through this valley in 1903, in 1908 the original Wisconsin Central built what is now the Superior Sub over the creek and Reserve branch shortly before the Soo Line lease of the WC (the Soo passed under the trestle where the road is today). Soo Line abandoned the branch in 1931. Like many structures around the WC, Soo Line lettering remained intact for many years, often outlasting the WC itself. February 16, 2003.

As part of the sale, WC granted C&NW trackage rights over its Valley and Superior Subs to allow it to continue to reach Itasca Yard from its own lines in central Wisconsin. Trains such as PRITA (Proviso, IL, to Itasca, WI) would connect off the C&NW Adams line with the WC Valley Sub at Necedah and proceed north to Junction City and switch to the WC Superior Sub for remainder of the trip north.

VALUABLE RAIL

The WC had a knack for being resourceful when it made a purchase, unneeded track was not simply abandoned and sold for scrap. There was a considerable amount of heavy ribbon rail (typically 1,300 feet in length) that C&NW had installed on portions of the line. That rail was gathered as the line was dismantled and dragged to Spooner. Once positioned at Spooner, a specialized winch car was borrowed from the C&NW and used to "thread" the lengths of rail up and onto strings of flat cars so the rail could be distributed for installation at other locations on the WC. During the summer of 1994, an SW1200 was used to retrieve rail as track was removed and for positioning of the flat cars that would haul the rail. To preserve rail access, the county would purchase the track from Springbrook to Spooner, later leasing it to the Wisconsin Great Northern.

Spooner was a long-standing division point on the C&NW route to the Twin Ports. After the WC purchase, the rails were silent for a while. In the summer of 1994, WC used Spooner as a base for removing the tracks between Rice Lake and Spooner. The heavy rail on the route would be reused elsewhere on the WC. WC 1235 was based out of Spooner for a time as lengths of rail were dragged to the Spooner Yard. At Spooner was a rail-loading machine borrowed from C&NW that allowed the lengths of rail to be loaded onto strings of flat cars for transport. On September 11, 1994, 1235 rests at the west end of the Spooner Yard with some 89-foot flat cars. Once these cars were loaded, they were moved to Hayward Jct. on the Superior Sub and forwarded to locations around the system.

Washburn County wanted to preserve railroad access to Spooner despite a dearth of traffic that resulted in WC planning to abandon the tracks. 18 miles of track were purchased by the state in 1998 from Spooner to Springbrook and managed by the Washburn County Rail Transit Commission. The county RTC has an operating agreement with the Wisconsin Great Northern Railroad to maintain this track and provide service. The WGN built their business around passenger excursions. A showpiece of their roster is this restored EMD F7 wearing a Great Northern-inspired scheme on a bright winter day in Spooner. March 16, 2002.

Aside from combining the routes, upgrading the Superior Sub also entailed expanding sidings and even constructing brand-new passing tracks. At the remote crossroads known as Hauer, a new siding was built. After a contest among employees to name the siding, the name Bigfoot was selected—it fit the deep-woods location well. It is not hard to imagine a lanky sasquatch emerging from the forest and striding across the tracks out here. As 1997 draws to a close, the east switch of Bigfoot siding has been placed and new ties distributed along the roadbed of the new track. In time, the Superior Sub would be outfitted with power switches and CTC signals as it developed into a high-capacity corridor. December 28, 1997.

Another new siding (8,003 feet long) was built at Hawthorne. This was built west of the old siding C&NW had at Hawthorne (only 3,287 feet). The old siding had its west switch removed and was converted into a stub track mainly for MOW use. In time (post-WC), the new switch seen here would be removed when CN converted the hill from here all the way west to South Itasca into double track. UP train PRITA provides a little extra variety with some borrowed CSX units. The lead unit CSX 8146 was originally purchased by the Louisville & Nashville. June 4, 2000.

A NEW JUNCTION

The only major customers in this area C&NW had were at Hayward, served via a remnant of the Bayfield line branching off at Trego. C&NW elected to retain the track to serve those mills and have a new connection with the WC Superior Sub built and christened "Hayward Jct." near where the two lines cross the Namekagon River and each other. The C&NW would run a train between Hayward and Wisconsin Rapids to tie this traffic into the rest of their network.

RICE LAKE SOUTH CONSOLIDATION

At the south end of this newly purchased line, WC had served customers at Rice Lake on its own track from Cameron via a remnant of the old SOO branch to Reserve, WI. It paralleled and crossed the C&NW south of Rice Lake. Since the C&NW was in better condition, the WC removed their Rice Lake Spur and utilized the ex-C&NW to reach Rice Lake including existing WC customers. Interestingly, on the north side of Cameron there was an intact siding, and between the two switches on the mainline there was the same heavy rail that had been harvested from the abandoned sections. It was removed from the mainline here as well. To avoid the missing rail, the switches were lined for the siding and spiked, making the trip through the siding the only option for trains running to and from Rice Lake.

FAR-REACHING RIPPLES

The reworking of the Superior Sub was an exciting development for the WC and demonstrated the new and creative paths they would take to keep growing the railroad. However, it could be argued that this development would come to influence the future of the WC more than any other move the railroad made during its independent years.

Opposite page:

Above: This remnant of the Soo Line branch through Rice Lake was still in use after the WC switched over to the ex-C&NW tracks to reach Rice Lake from Cameron. Besse Lumber Company's Birchwood Manufacturing received carloads of logs at their facility in downtown Rice Lake just beyond this bridge spanning the Red Cedar River. The local will loop around to a connection with the old C&NW main and run around the two empty log cars for the trip back to Cameron. October 4, 2001.

Below: Three high-horsepower locomotives (two UP and one SOO) work to lift a heavy potash train out of the Lake Superior basin on the ex-C&NW portion of the Superior Sub. This location of Rockmont is where the DSS&A once crossed over the Omaha and paralleled it roughly a quarter mile to the west on the way down the hill, until the nearby section of the DSS&A was abandoned in 1935. October 11, 1998.

JUNCTION
400 FEET
BEGIN
CTC

C&NW trackage rights trains offered some variety on the Valley and Superior Sub. After the 1995 merger with Union Pacific, UP locomotives meant armour yellow would show up on this route as well. More models and paint schemes showed up once Union Pacific merged with Southern Pacific in 1996. Case in point is the PRITA on September 7, 1998 passing through Auburndale, WI. Cotton Belt (St. Louis Southwestern) 7797 still wears its as-delivered paint but has lost some of its distinctive SP light package and dogleg "L" window on the engineer's side of the cab. Trailing is an EMD "tunnel motor" repainted into UP colors, a model emblematic of the SP, Denver Rio Grande & Western, and Cotton Belt.

Opposite page:

Above: The UP trackage rights trains reached Superior by traversing the Valley and Superior Subs. Here at the appropriately named Junction City, a UP train makes the transition from the Valley Sub onto the Superior Sub. This trains northward route on the Valley Sub utilized the southwest quadrant connection leading to the CTC siding west of the Junction City crossing of the two subdivisions. A pair of UP SD40-2s bracket a Conrail SD60M on the move out the siding. April 13, 1997.

Below: Searchlights protect the east end of the Medford Sub where it joins the Superior Sub. Originally the mainline, the old route from Ashland steadily faded in importance compared to the new route the train is on. The cutoff from Spencer to Owen was not built until 1910, four years after the line from Owen to Ladysmith was put in. As has been the case ever since, priority traffic to the Twin Cities and Twin Ports keeps the rails polished in that direction. Hinting at a major commodity routed over the Superior Sub are the iron ore pellets found on Clark St. In the coming years, the Medford Sub would lose a little more stature with this CTC junction removed and the tracks tied into the sidetracks at left only (connecting with the Superior Sub at a manual switch east of the grain elevator). Train L063 rolls west on the Superior Sub on April 12, 1997.

5

WC ACQUIRES GB&W AND FRVR

The WC had grown and developed within its original footprint and had a record of success by the early 1990s. Expansion of the "WC model" would get its first growth opportunity with the acquisition of two other Wisconsin carriers. By 1993 Itel Corporation owned one of the oldest Wisconsin railroads, Green Bay & Western, and one of the newest, Fox River Valley Railroad, and both were up for sale.

THE GREEN BAY ROUTE

The Green Bay and Western had a colorful history bridging east and west across Wisconsin. From railroad car ferries with traffic off lower Michigan lines Ann Arbor Railroad and Pere Marquette Railway to connections with western carriers like Chicago Great Western, Chicago Burlington and Quincy, Chicago Milwaukee St. Paul & Pacific, and Chicago & North Western at Winona, MN, the GB&W had a varied book of business serving both local traffic and bridge traffic for other roads. The GB&W remained independent through the turbulent 1980s, the Burlington Northern had made a serious attempt to purchase the GB&W. The BN takeover would not come to pass, and by the 1990s, the Itel Corporation was growing weary of operating the GB&W and the Fox River Valley Railroad. Packaging them together would likely sweeten the deal and garner more and better offers. The GB&W still had a respectable traffic base, although it no longer reached Kewanee on the east end nor Winona, MN, on the west. By 1993, the roster (consisting exclusively of American Locomotive Company "ALCO" locomotives) was a definite anomaly among even short-line and regional railroads.

To the Wisconsin Central, a purchase of the Green Bay & Western presented opportunities given the proximity of the various customers and connections to the core WC service area. It would provide WC with a route into Green Bay over a line they previously traversed via trackage rights from Black Creek (on WC's Shawano Sub) to reach Titletown. GB&W paper mill customers in Biron and Wisconsin Rapids were right in the backyard of WC's Steven Point hub and could easily be served as often as needed with traffic funneled directly onto the WC mainline. Farther west on the GB&W were some steady customers such as Badger Mining at Taylor and Ashley Furniture at Arcadia, along with the outlet to interchange with Burlington Northern at East Winona, WI.

In contrast to the locomotives of the GB&W, WC hung on to specialized pieces of equipment like the X190 Jordan spreader/snowplow. Seen here at Rhinelander on August 23, 1997.

Unlike the core of the WC mainline, the GB&W was a "dark" mainline operated using track warrants without lineside signals. Exceptions were places where the GB&W connected with or crossed other railroads. For example, at Merrillan, WI, looking east down the old GB&W, a stop signal displayed on this searchlight protects against the conflicting move by a westbound Union Pacific manifest. February 6, 1999.

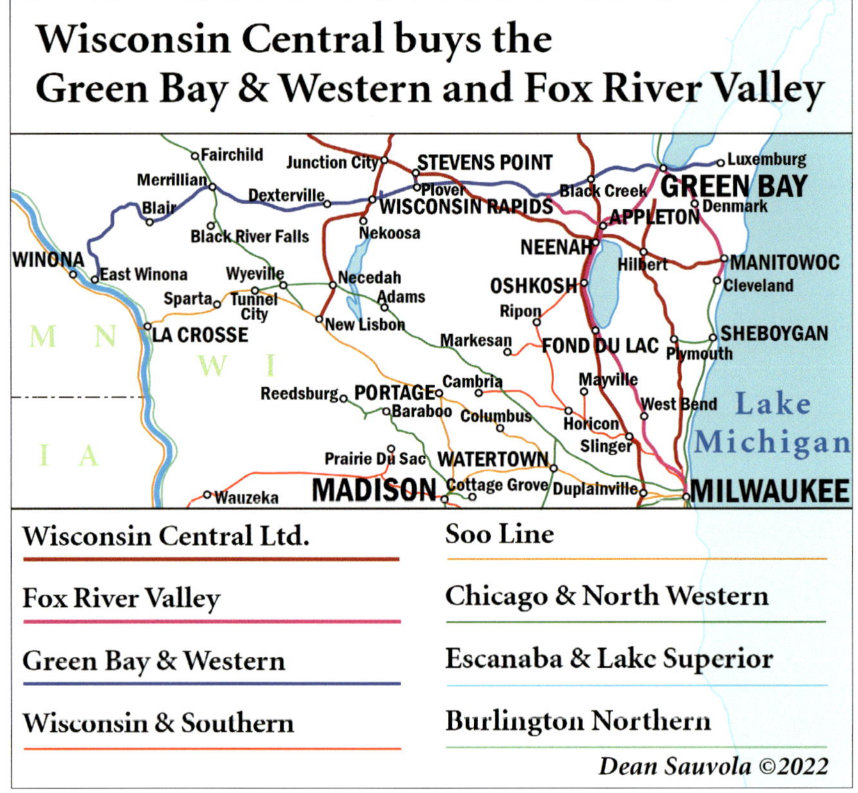

THE SHORT-LIVED "FEVER"

By the mid-1980s, the Chicago & North Western was intent on selling off their operations north of the Milwaukee metro area through Green Bay and into Upper Michigan. The C&NW had its hands full with new operations in the booming Wyoming Powder River Basin coal field. The sale would be conducted in two segments, "Duck Creek North" and "Duck Creek South." Duck Creek was a somewhat arbitrary dividing line just north of the large North Green Bay Yard where the lines to Wausau and Marinette diverged. In 1988, a deal was completed to sell "Duck Creek South" to Itel Corporation (owners of the Green Bay & Western). As it turned out "Duck Creek North" did not sell and would stay in the fold for the rest of the C&NW's existence.

Itel named the new operation the Fox River Valley Railroad, reporting marks FRVR, commonly known by fans of the operation as the "Fever." The two traffic staples on this line were local paper traffic from the mills in Green Bay and around Appleton as well as overhead trains, PRANA and ANPRA, which connected the now-isolated operation north of Green Bay with Proviso Yard (Chicago). The new railroad struggled with debt and never really found its footing, after a time it was placed under a common management with the Green Bay & Western, but that only helped so much. Unlike the GB&W, the FRVR roster consisted of secondhand EMD locomotives. They had decades of hard service even before their time on the FRVR, but the parts and familiarity around the WC shops meant they had a brighter future with the WC than the GB&W power did.

A couple of EMD SD24s came with the Fox River Valley purchase, among a handful of units in FRVR colors. Never a common model, SD24s were very rare by the time they made it onto the WC roster. The SD24s saw service all over the WC especially on locals and branch lines. On July 20, 1996, the 2401 rests at the Marquette roundhouse with borrowed DM&IR SD9.

WC's purchase of the Fox River Valley Railroad included plenty of ex-C&NW track and ex-C&NW locomotives. Most of the ex-C&NW units wore a hasty patch during their time on the FRVR. As seen on the cab of GP30 number 820, the C&NW logo was emerging through an old patch with newer WC initials reflecting the current ownership. May 12, 1996.

Built as C&NW 1547 in April 1951, 4505 was among the oldest locomotives to come with the Fox River Valley purchase. During its long career on the C&NW, it received a short hood and new number before going to FRVR as part of the line sale. With minimal remarking, it would soldier on for WC. Unlike the GP30s and GP35s, these first-generation Geeps would not be repainted during their time on the WC. Wisconsin Rapids, April 5, 1998.

WC 2556 is an ex-FRVR GP35 seen after repainting and renumbering (formerly WC 831) working the former Green Bay & Western. At Taylor, WI FL077 switches the small yard where carloads of industrial sand were received off the Badger Mining Corporation spur to their mine north of town. Sand loads were long a staple of the traffic on this line predating the frac sand boom that would occur about a decade later. July 29, 2001.

ANPRA is passing the depot of the namesake city of the West Bend Sub. In addition to the three new AC4400CWs up front is one of the ex-FRVR SD24s making another trip over "home rails." With the abandonment of much of the line, this location would change dramatically. The mainline would become the Eisenbahn State Trail, the Museum of Wisconsin Art would be built across from the depot, and the depot would eventually be renovated for use by the Ozaukee Washington Land Trust. December 2, 1995.

The Fox River Valley Railroad had a lot to offer a growing WC, not just in terms of additional customers but even more so in how the physical plant could be integrated with the busiest parts of the WC. By the time Chicago-bound traffic reached Neenah, it was flowing from the west, from the north, and even the east out of Sault Ste. Marie. In places, Oshkosh in particular, the WC mainline was ill-suited to handle this flood of traffic. The old SOO route was bedeviled by street-running, sharp curves, and an aged swing bridge over the Fox River. Although the FRVR bridge across the Fox also dated back to the 1800s, the rest of the route was a much straighter shot better suited to modern freight operations. In Fond du Lac as well, the FRVR operated an ex-C&NW yard that practically mirrored WC's own Shops Yard. By adding a few connections WC could essentially double the capacity of a major hub overnight. Along with the upgrades that could be made to the core of the WC's network, they would gain another direct line to Green Bay (more direct than the GB&W main) and a line south to north suburban Milwaukee.

PURCHASE HAPPENS UNDER THE FOX VALLEY & WESTERN BANNER

With good reasons to find both properties attractive, WC moved ahead with a purchase. This was the first large expansion of the WC; as such, management was careful not to grow in a way that would reclassify the railroad as a Class I in the eyes of the ICC. The purchase of the GB&W and FRVR was done as a new entity called the Fox Valley & Western. For the most part, this was an invisible "paper" railroad apart from the name showing up on some property signs inside the familiar WC shield.

Train ANPRA has almost reached its destination of Butler Yard as it cuts across the north side of Milwaukee. ANPRA has been on Union Pacific rails since just before Granville, WI. This was the signature train of the FRVR during its short existence and would be a carryover for the WC's Fox Valley & Western until the purchase of the UP tracks north of Green Bay in 1997. December 16, 1995.

With the Green Bay & Western purchase WC gained another location to interchange with BNSF, along the Mississippi River at East Winona, WI. With turns based out of Merrillan, the daily train would go east in the evening and turn back at Stevens Point at night. At Merrillan, a fresh crew would come on duty and head west in the wee hours of the morning. On summer days, FL078 would be ready to go east after working the BNSF interchange around sunup. WC 3009 greets the morning as it crosses Wisconsin Highway 35 at the tiny locale of Marshland. This is the first crossing as the line transitions from the broad Mississippi River Valley to the Trempealeau River Valley which it will follow for roughly half the distance to Wisconsin Rapids. July 31, 2001.

Once the deal closed, changes began right away. GB&W's yard and shops at Norwood Yard in Green Bay were shuttered in favor of the FRVR's ex-C&NW facilities at North Green Bay. From a newly rebuilt connection at Amherst Junction to Plover, the GB&W mainline was abandoned with traffic routed through Stevens Point. From Plover west, the GB&W stayed mostly intact with regular service continuing out to the west end at East Winona. The FRVR route into Green Bay was the preferred routing for WC traffic right away. Eventually most of the GB&W east of Plover would be abandoned.

The fleet of American Locomotive Company "ALCOs" were parked right away, with only a few instances of select units pressed into service shortly after the sale to get through brief traffic surges, then sold to short-line operations. Some of the ALCOs found a new home at the Minnesota Commercial Railway in the Twin Cities. The Minnesota Commercial even traded a pair of EMD SW1500s to the WC in the deal. The GB&W had maintained the ALCOs well despite their age and some went right into service in full GB&W garb. In fact, the Minnesota Commercial liked those GB&W colors so much they would take on a very similar livery for future repaints of all their power.

Like the old GB&W property, changes to the old FRVR started right away. With a connection at Winnebago north of Oshkosh, the ex-C&NW towards Fond du Lac would become the preferred route and the old SOO used as a backup for overflow traffic. More connections south of Oshkosh allowed for greater operational flexibility and essentially double track where the two lines parallel each other through Van Dyne. In time, the SOO route through downtown Oshkosh would be abandoned in favor of the ex-C&NW. South of Fond du Lac, the West Bend Sub

Train 119 for Green Bay bisects the fields of Wrightstown, WI, on this ex-FRVR/ex-C&NW route. Among the ways WC now had to reach Green Bay, this quickly became the preferred line. It was not common to find the F45s paired up on a train (or in this case F45-FP45), but it sure was a neat looking lashup when it did happen. In this view you can also see the extra length of the FP45 that once accommodated a steam generator early in its career when it pulled passenger trains on the Santa Fe. April 6, 1996.

Unlike the well-worn RSD15s, much of the GB&W's roster was still in good shape thanks to the shop forces at Norwood Yard in Green Bay. Twin Cities terminal road Minnesota Commercial was a safe harbor for second-hand ALCOs and a ready buyer for several of the GB&W units. A pair of C424s went right to work on the Minnesota Commercial without even minimal remarking for their new owner. 313 and 314 work the yard at New Brighton, where the WC interchanged daily. The Minnesota Commercial liked the look of the GB&W power enough that they would adopt a closely inspired scheme for future repaints of all their power. March 27, 1994.

Among the more obscure units to see service on the Fox River Valley Railroad were some ex-LS&I ALCO RSD15 "Alligators" that sister road GB&W picked up after their retirement on the LS&I. Originally these six-axle units belonged to the Santa Fe before LS&I picked them up in the 1970s. They had no future on the WC and no potential buyers. Aside from the 2407, which was donated to the Illinois Railway Museum, these units were scraped on site at the North Green Bay roundhouse. In a somber scene, LS&I paint is visible on the outside of some electrical cabinets along with concrete ballast weights left over from the scraped units. April 6, 1996.

stayed in place as a through route, almost exclusively to continue the routing of trains ANPRA/PRANA between C&NW's isolated track to the north and the rest of their system. The piece of the old C&NW Shoreline route was served by a local out of Green Bay as far as Denmark with the segment from there to Rockwood abandoned.

The EMD power from the FRVR fared much better than GB&W's fleet with the new owner. Even the rare models such as SD24s and the lone SD35 would go on to spend years powering trains around the WC system, many seeing rebuilds and fresh paint in time. Some ex-LS&I RSD15s had seen limited use on the FRVR, and although one was donated to the Illinois Railway Museum (GB&W 2407), the balance of them would be scrapped on-site at the North Green Bay roundhouse.

LONG GOODBYES

It was with mixed emotions that long-term fans of the Green Bay & Western watched the transformation of perhaps Wisconsin's most distinctive railroad. It seemed a unique society and culture built on multi-generational railroad families vanished overnight. On the other hand, this deal contributed a lot to the core of WC's growing operation, making them the dominant player in northeastern Wisconsin.

A pair of GP40s head west down the Whitehall Sub at Hixton, WI, beneath some spring rain clouds at the end of the day. One of the main customers on the west end of the old Green Bay & Western is Badger Mining at Taylor, WI. A cut of two-bay covered hoppers for sand hauling can be seen at the front of the train. April 28, 2000.

Just south of their respective yards at North Fond du Lac, the SOO and C&NW both crossed the Fond du Lac River on parallel bridges. The through truss bridge on the ex-FRVR was near the start of the West Bend Sub leading through downtown Fond du Lac. One of the new SP locomotives leads train ANPRA as it begins a morning trip to Butler Yard in Milwaukee. December 2, 1995.

With a grand passenger station and extensive platforms, the past importance C&NW's Air Line Subdivision once held is evident. Passenger trains have not called since before Amtrak was created and more recently this was the mainline of the humble Fox River Valley Railroad. After purchasing the FRVR, WC ran the train seen here, ANPRA, to connect C&NW (later UP) traffic between Green Bay and Milwaukee. In early 1997, once WC purchased Union Pacific's lines north of Green Bay, this last bit of through traffic came off the Air Line. It would become a stub to Eden from the north and a stub to West Bend on the south end with the middle portion abandoned. Eden would be served from a connection on the south end of town and the track seen here through central Fond du Lac would be removed as well. August 24, 1996.

The versatile four-axle EMD Geeps that joined the roster when WC purchased the FRVR saw extensive use all over the system. 2252 is headed up the Plymouth Sub on L027. It is a pleasant fall evening just south of Cedarburg on November 12, 1998.

A DM&IR ore train with run-through power crosses the ex-C&NW swing bridge at Oshkosh, WI. The SD38 still wears the orange of the Elgin, Joliet & Eastern. EJ&E and DM&IR were sibling railroads under common ownership who traded locomotives on occasion as requirements shifted on the two properties. In time, WC, DM&IR, and EJ&E would all be under the CN umbrella. March 23, 1996.

The old FRVR mainline south of Fond du Lac gave WC three parallel north–south routes in southeastern Wisconsin. The Chicago Sub handled the lion's share of the traffic while the Plymouth Sub was not used for through traffic but had enough steady customers online to warrant a local working the line for the duration of WC's existence. The West Bend Sub was the odd line out with very limited online customers and, once the WC purchased the UP operations north of Green Bay, had no need to host the ANPRA/PRANA trains. A large segment would be abandoned from Eden to West Bend once the through trains were removed.

A pigeon overlooks the year plate on the 1899-built swing bridge over the Fox River at Oshkosh. This line quickly became the preferred route for WC traffic through Oshkosh once purchased from Fox River Valley Railroad. The venerable bridge would serve for another seventeen years before being replaced by a new bascule bridge on the same alignment. March 23, 1996.

WC 6529 approaches Black Wolf West on the ex-FRVR line on November 30, 2000. By this time, the two mainlines between Oshkosh and Fond du Lac were integrated with a crossover to the old SOO main at Black Wolf West, another crossover at Black Wolf East, and two main tracks for the 8.4 miles between Black Wolf West and Shops West. At left can be seen the code line along the SOO main now abandoned here. Just west of here, at a switch called Airport, is another connection to the old SOO main where it is used as an industrial spur to serve remaining customers on the south side of Oshkosh including Oshkosh Corporation (heavy trucks).

As shabby as much of the FRVR power was when WC bought the railroad, power such as the GP30s shone like a new penny after getting a fresh coat of paint. 2252 crosses the Iron River south of Mellen where it empties into the Bad River headed railroad west on the Ashland Sub. With standard Blomberg trucks, WC saw a bright future for the three ex-FRVR GP30s; the ex-SOO GP30s had been on the WC from the start, but the trade-in ALCO trucks they rode on were becoming a maintenance issue. September 15, 1995.

Between the south side of Oshkosh and North Fond du Lac, WC built three crossovers between the parallel ex-FRVR and WC mainlines. Just south of Subway Road, a new crossover at Shops West allowed trains to access the ex-FRVR yard from the ex-SOO mainline. In this view, a westbound T009 is departing from the ex-FRVR side and crossing over to the ex-SOO side. At either Black Wolf East or Black Wolf West, this train would cross back over to the ex-FRVR main to pass through Oshkosh. August 24, 1996.

6

OPPORTUNITIES AND PARTNERSHIPS:
WC Takes Over Operations of the Algoma Central

The Algoma Central has long been known around the Midwest and central Canada as the "route of the black bear" with their popular excursion trains to Agawa Canyon north of Sault Ste. Marie, ON.

ROUTE OF THE BLACK BEAR

The Algoma Central was constructed relatively late to supply the industries at Sault Ste. Marie with raw materials, lumber, and iron ore. In the early days of the twentieth century, the railroad was building north and intended to reach Hudson Bay but ultimately ended at Hearst, Ontario, with a connection to the National Transcontinental Railway. The company steadily diversified their business with substantial investments in related enterprises such as ships, trucking, and resource-rich real estate. In time, these other areas became more profitable than the railroad.

The route of the railroad crossed a scenic wilderness with a local passenger train providing access to many remote lakes and camps between Sault Ste. Marie and Hearst—better known was the Agawa Canyon tour train, which became an institution over the years and major tourist draw in the Canadian Soo. While the tour trains were long and well patronized, the local covering the whole line required years of subsidies from the government to offset operating losses.

In 1995, a deal was reached where the Wisconsin Central purchased the Algoma Central under the umbrella of new subsidiary Wisconsin Central Canada Holdings. WC continued to operate the local and tour trains. For three years, iron ore continued to be shipped by rail from the mine at Wawa, up a branch to Hawk Jct., then south to the steel mill at the Soo. A great deal could be written and illustrated covering the Algoma Central, but for the purposes of this book, I will focus on the impact this purchase had on the WC's operations in the U.S., particularly the locomotive assets the WC gained through the deal. Also, the fleet of notable power WC attained specifically for use on the Algoma Central passenger trains.

When the WC started, EMD SD40-2s were the gold standard for mainline power on railroads across the U.S. and Canada and commanded top dollar if they were available. The discounted price on used SD45s meant they would be the core of the WC fleet. With the Algoma Central purchase WC would add five SD40-2s to their roster (and 1 SD40). These locomotives were popular for a reason and after a quick pass through the shops to address a few items, including WC logos on the nose and new numbers, they were put right to work. WC 6003, formerly AC 185, on T050 basks in the morning sun at Byron, WI, March 23, 1996.

Although outnumbered on the WC, there were times when enough AC power converged that you might mistake Wisconsin for Ontario. At daybreak on the "FRVR side" of North Fond du Lac, Lakeshore Drive crossing, two SD40-2s meet. WC 6002 is on a parked westbound train. WC 6003 is on T050 that will cross over to the "WC side" just ahead on the way to Byron Hill. March 23, 1996.

A notable aspect of the Algoma Central operation was their passenger trains, both long-distance service to Hearst and the popular day excursion train to Agawa Canyon. In a surprising move, WC put together a fleet of classic streamlined EMD FP9 A and F9 B units to power these passenger trains. The Fs got their own paint scheme with full Algoma Central lettering. The dedicated locomotives allowed WC to disperse the versatile GP38-2s to tasks all over the system. The Fs mainly stayed on the AC mainline running north from Sault Ste. Marie, Ontario, except in the winter when the off season lessened the passenger traffic. Winter offered the chance to find the Fs supplementing freight power on the WC, although normally only as far as Gladstone, MI, before returning to the Canadian Soo. Two of the Algoma Central FP9s layover at Gladstone on January 18, 1997.

Beyond the locomotives acquired with the Algoma Central purchase, there were the freight cars, another valuable addition to the growing railroad. Algoma Central bulkhead gondolas moving pulpwood, and hopper cars moving ballast then iron ore pellets, alternating seasonally, would become a common sight around the WC. AC 1266 brings a load east at New Richmond, WI, on March 5, 2004.

SL087, the local that worked north out of Green Bay over the Marinette Sub, is working the small yard at Marinette, WI. Positioned next to the mainline is an old Fairbanks Morse coal elevator from the days of steam power. The Algoma Central GP38-2s looked great even with the WC logo added to reflect the new ownership. July 2, 1999.

The spotting details of the Algoma Central locomotives left little doubt about their Canadian origins, the shape of the handrails, the location of the class lights, the bell between the number boards, etc. However, they looked great even after receiving a fresh coat of Wisconsin Central colors. For example, WC 2006 is very spiffy with its own look as the logo shares space on the nose with the headlights. Seen here on the stub at Ladysmith between trips powering the Barron Sub local. September 4, 2000.

WC 6006 teams up with two SD45s as they hustle train T012 up the Shawano Sub, just geographically west/railroad east of Shawano. This train surely includes cars bound for 6006's old stomping grounds of Sault Ste. Marie. Algoma Central's classic paint scheme was similar enough to go well with WC units, but the big six-axle power would look terrific once painted to match the rest of the fleet. December 21, 1996.

Perhaps the most transformed of the ex-AC locomotives were the GP7s. Half of their eight GP7s had been rebuilt in 1978 and designated GP7Rs, but all of them would receive a full overhaul by WC with plenty of upgrades including chopped noses. Typical of the road-switching tasks they would perform all over the WC, 1503 is seen switching the coal track at the Rhinelander paper mill on December 27, 1999.

A couple of the FP9s team up with an SDL39 to move train L035 east over the Manistique Sub. Seen here crossing the Manistique River at its namesake city. Before the Algoma Central purchase, this was the SOO Sub, but once the ACR SOO Sub from Sault Ste. Marie north was part of the fold, this became the Manistique Sub to avoid confusion. January 18, 1997.

6652
WISCONSIN CENTRAL
WISCONSIN CENTRAL 6599
SOO LINE
14'

WISCONSIN CENTRAL 6617
SOO LINE
14'

The fostering of intermodal traffic was not unique to WC, but there were aspects to that service that stand out. The idea of more frequent and faster service was evident in how WC built up a robust trailer on flat-car traffic between Green Bay and Chicago. Conventional wisdom on Class One railroads was that an intermodal haul needed to be a minimum of 400 miles to compete with trucks and be worth the effort, the Green Bay to Chicago route was roughly half that distance. Undeterred, WC worked closely with shippers in Green Bay and connecting railroads in Chicago to win over a steadily increasing share of the paper and tissue loads. A pair of SD45s hustle T241 out of Sussex and under the Bug Line Trail, built on the grade of Milwaukee Road's abandoned branch to North Lake. July 1, 1997.

Opposite page:

Above: WC moved a lot of iron ore pellets destined for steel mills as far away as Utah, mostly through the Chicago gateway. One of the more unique ore moves was the seasonal haul of pellets from the Minorca Mine in Minnesota to the dock at Escanaba, MI. The dock at Escanaba was not subject to the wintertime closure of the Soo Locks like the ports on Lake Superior, allowing the pellets to continue to be delivered by boat to the lower lake mills. This routing was a joint effort by DM&IR, WC and C&NW (later UP). Originally the trains travelled via the DM&IR from the mine to Superior, the C&NW from Superior to Cameron, the WC from Cameron to Hermansville, and finally the C&NW again from Hermansville to Escanaba. After WC bought the C&NW route south of Superior WC handled the move from Superior to Hermansville via Ladysmith. Once the Flambeau Mine in Ladysmith closed and its ore was no longer sent east over the Bradley and Pembine Subs, these wintertime Minorca trains were the only traffic some portions of the line would host. At Goodman, WI, OSTES-5, a loaded Minorca train for Escanaba crosses over Highway 8 on February 6, 2000.

Below: The Minorca trains used cars from C&NW's long-serving fleet of ore cars. The trip to and from Minnesota was an arduous journey, especially when loaded, coming across the saw-tooth profile of the old Soo Line. Aged brittle draft gear could be prone to cause pull-aparts on these trips, so WC turned to running a manned helper on the rear of these trains to help shepherd them over the road. A solo engineer was placed in the cab of the lead locomotive and one in the helper engine. Here the helper engine pushes on the rear of this heavy train keeping the cars "bunched" to insure a smooth trip. February 6, 2000.

There was a variety of trackage rights arrangements on WC; SOO/CP rock trains on the Dresser Sub, SOO/CP access to the Weston power plant from New Lisbon, UP trains to Superior, WSOR from Slinger to Waukesha, and one that bridged Wisconsin and Michigan. Trackage rights from Pembine, WI, to North Escanaba, MI, were established to maintain the connection between the Escanaba & Lake Superior Railroad shop at Escanaba and their mainline once service over the original mainline to Channing was suspended. Operating on an irregular as-needed basis, these trains took the Pembine Sub all the way to North Escanaba when they started. Later, once WC purchased the Union Pacific trackage in the area, they would take the Bradley Sub (as the track through Pembine was then designated) to Hermansville where they would get on the Iron Mountain Sub, at Powers they would take the Marinette Sub to Algoma Jct. then North Escanaba. Despite the number of junctions and connections the newer route covered roughly the same distance. On December 23, 1995, E&LS 300 waits to copy a warrant for its one-car train to enter the Pembine Sub at Pembine and proceed east to North Escanaba.

A major coup for the WC was had in partnership with the Southern Pacific. Geneva Steel was a large mill built during World War II in Utah just south of Salt Lake City. By the 1980s, iron sources local to the mill were depleted and ore was brought in from greater distances. Union Pacific had the most logical route for ore to travel from the Minnesota Iron Range via connections over the C&NW. Given the distances via Chicago, it was unlikely WC could be a player. A unique strategy, however, did enable WC and SP to win the contract. By using steel coal cars to move the ore, they were able to backhaul coal loads from Utah and Colorado to the Midwest. Having revenue in both directions enabled the longer routing to work. In the mid-1990s, SP bolstered its locomotive fleet, first with 101 new GE Dash 9-44CWs built in 1994 then 279 AC4400CWs in 1995. Seemingly overnight, brand-new power, freshly delivered, appeared all over the WC, both hauling the Geneva ore trains and used on many other runs between ore train assignments. Low December afternoon light illuminates a few shiny new SP engines on an ore load at Duplainville, WI. December 9, 1995.

An interesting development saw regular passenger service return to a portion of the WC in 1996. Metra built out their new "North Central Service" on the WC Chicago Sub from a connection at Franklin Park up to Antioch just short of the state line. Along with hosting the rush-hour trains came quite a bit of investment including double tracking of the corridor and signal upgrades. This portion of the railroad had not seen passenger service since Soo Line's Laker in 1965 and had not hosted commuter trains since the 1890s. WC 6578 west passes the under-construction Antioch Metra station with T051 on November 24, 1995.

The C&NW hands off a loaded coal train bound for Green Bay or Weston, WI, to a WC crew here at the Minnesota Commercial yard in New Brighton, MN. The C&NW GEs were the pushers on the rear of the coal train. Now that they have cut off, the WC power will tie on and lead the train east out of the MNNR yard, then over the CP Withrow Sub to Withrow where WC rails will take the train the rest of the way to the power plant. March 1, 1995.

The generating station at Weston was a landmark and a major destination on the Valley Sub. Especially evident on a brisk winter day when great clouds of steam would rise over the plant. WC 587 leads T012 from Wausau to Stevens Point past Weston on February 17, 2001.

Junction City was the place where the SOO mainline and Milwaukee Road Valley Line crossed. Once the SOO bought the Milwaukee, it gained a new importance for trains serving the industries around central Wisconsin and that relevance only increased under Wisconsin Central. The WC would restore the northwest connection allowing movements in all directions from either line. The northeast connection from Wausau to Stevens Point saw plenty of moves such as this run making its way onto the Superior Sub. WC 587 was repainted early and did not hold up as well as later paintjobs. By this late in its time on WC, you can plainly see the black and orange of the original owner, Milwaukee Road, showing through the WC colors. February 17, 2001.

7

WC PURCHASES THE UNION PACIFIC LINES IN NORTHEAST WISCONSIN AND UPPER MICHIGAN

In the 1980s C&NW spun off its line from Milwaukee to Green Bay. It also intended to spin off the rest of its track from Green Bay north and came very close to doing just that. With a reprieve the "Duck Creek North" lines stayed in the fold into the 1990s and under the Union Pacific flag after 1995. The track was profitable but an outlier from UP's core business. Finally, in early 1997 WC closed on a deal to purchase the 207 miles of track from UP.

A NATURAL FIT

The early history and impetus for constructing a railroad can hamstring the modern operation with circuitous connections and extra miles. This was the case for WC, especially in northeast Wisconsin and Upper Michigan. The Soo Line and the DSS&A both built their mainlines on an east–west axis across this territory, their only direct connections to each other were found at the east end in Trout Lake and Sault Ste. Marie. Despite more traffic evolving into a north–south flow over the decades, Soo Line and then WC had to put on lots of extra miles via Trout Lake to reach the core of their system—a distinct disadvantage compared to trucks which had their choice of highways leading directly south.

Over time, the lines that did run north–south in Upper Michigan mostly withered and were abandoned or fell out of service and nature started to reclaim the right of ways. The exception was C&NW's "Ore Line" from Ishpeming to Escanaba, which moved iron ore pellets south to the dock and was maintained to high standards to keep that heavy tonnage fluid. Not only was the route attractive, but the trackage served large customers at Empire Mine as well as two paper mills near Iron Mountain (Quinnesec and Niagara).

Traffic feeding the WC lines in central and eastern Upper Michigan from the hubs of Stevens Point or Fond du Lac came up the Shawano Sub to Argonne. Compared to the Shawano Sub, the ex-C&NW through Marinette, WI, Menominee, MI, and Powers offered another attractive short-cut.

With a backdrop of the large tailings piles that comprise the northern edge of the Empire Mine, a pair of SD45s lift a train of Empire Mine pellets out of Empire Jct. Given track capacities and grades around the mine, normal practice was to bring out the loaded cars in two cuts of fifty-four cars. At nearby Partridge Siding a road train of 108 cars would be assembled for the trip to Escanaba, MI. 7551 was unique on the roster with "Customer Minded Employees" spelled out in script on both sides of the long hood. September 5, 1998.

When the Empire Mine was in full production, the WC ran three ore trains a day out of Escanaba. Call times of the SORE trains were timed to allow one to be on the way back to Escanaba when the next one started its trip, resulting in a meet at Little Lake, Brampton, or arriving back at the ore yard just ahead of the next trains departure. At daybreak on a fine fall day SORE1 (Sault Ste. Marie Bridge Co.—ORE—1st train of the day) travels the placid edge of Goose Lake. October 2, 2001.

The most significant bridge on the Ore Sub was the aged through truss structure over the Escanaba River and the E&LS just beyond the yard limits for the ore yard. Extra piers can be seen where the C&NW reinforced this structure years ago. At one time, the streetcar line to Gladstone crossed under this bridge on their own bridge long since removed. March 23, 1997.

SORE2 arrives at Empire Jct. on its way from Escanaba, MI, to the Empire Mine. The 7500 series number of 7512 indicates this SD45 has cycled through the rebuild/upgrade program WC performed on these locomotives even though it continues to sport the V-stripe paintjob dating back to the early years of the WC. October 4, 1998.

The only diamond crossing between the WC and UP's ex-C&NW lines was found at Hermansville, MI. A modest but regular interchange occurred here between the two railroads via a connection in the southeast quadrant. On June 3, 1996, UP train ANPRA has just dropped a cut of boxcars for the WC with the power returning west to its train over the diamond. This crossing was "dark" and not signaled but instead required trains to stop clear of the crossing and proceed once it was safe to do so. In the wake of WC purchasing the UP track, the diamond would be removed and the old Soo Line route from here to Escanaba abandoned.

The WC sale was closing in and some railroader remarked this ore car in jest "WC 112307," seen on an Escanaba-bound ore train EPESO. Indeed, in about a month, these cars and this track would be bought by WC. It would ultimately turn out that there would be no ore cars marked WC. WC made the purchase under their Sault Ste. Marie Bridge Co. division and when the cars were remarked they would wear the SSAM reporting mark. Beaver, MI, December 23, 1996.

Wigwag crossing signals were a rare find by the late 1990s, but a handful remained on the Marinette Sub south of Powers when WC bought the line from UP. Train SOFD splits a pair of the warning devices at Daggett, MI, on February 6, 2000.

The route through Marinette, WI, and Menominee, MI, provided another link between WC and E&LS. Predecessor Milwaukee Road had long since abandoned its own crossing of the Menominee River in favor of using the parallel C&NW bridge. The connection near the south shore of the river lasted until the owners were the WC and E&LS. A major road project and realignment would see the E&LS Marinette depot moved a block south and the removal of roughly 2,000 feet of E&LS track. The E&LS/WC connection would be moved from near the river to the siding in front of the WC depot. On July 2, 1999, E&LS 202 (ex-Calumet & Hecla Mining) traverses the brand-new link between the railroads.

Put another way, a carload moved by WC from Ishpeming, MI, to Neenah, WI, in 1996 had to travel roughly 250 miles farther than it would in 1997 once WC routed traffic over the newly acquired route.

As with the Fox Valley & Western, this purchase would be done as separate division to keep WC regulated as a regional carrier and not bump the whole railroad into Class I status. WC made the purchase under the auspices of the Sault Sainte Marie Bridge Company, this subsidiary was a very old company established in 1887 to build and operate the international link between Sault Ste. Marie, MI, and Sault Ste. Marie, Ont. With only 1.2 miles of track, the bridge company had plenty of room to grow. Although the distinction was mostly on paper, the SSAM reporting mark started showing up on various pieces of rolling stock, particularly the fleet of ex-C&NW ore cars once they visited WC's car shop. Crews would soon bestow the nickname "Super Sams" on any cars bearing the SSAM reporting mark.

MORE STREAMLINING

WC had shipped a lot of iron ore, but this would be the first mine they served directly from the pocket and stockpiles at Empire Mine to the dock at Escanaba several times a day. The purchase meant drastic changes for the Newberry, Pembine, and Shawano Subs as through traffic was lost with long stretches of each taken out of service. The existing WC and expanded SSAM came together at Negaunee, Larch, and Hermansville, MI, along with Green Bay, WI (Duck Creek). Connections between the major yards at Gladstone and Escanaba would be a focus since the Larch interchange was rather sharply curved and sloped from the WC up to the ex-C&NW. Seeking an efficient and high-capacity route for traffic between Sault Ste. Marie and Green Bay, a brand-new connection was built between the old SOO mainline and the ex-C&NW on the west side of Escanaba. Algoma Junction allowed overhead traffic to and from the east to bypass the ore yards and use the Pembine Sub bridge over the Escanaba River on the way to Gladstone. WC could also serve the ore line from Gladstone by crossing the Escanaba River twice and looping through Escanaba before heading towards Negaunee. Although the Minneapolis–Sault Ste. Marie mainline was severed in Wisconsin shortly after the WC started up, this marked the first time the route was cut in Michigan. From the new connection near Algoma Jct. to Hermansville, the Pembine Sub would be abandoned. The connection at Hermansville was in the southeast quadrant of that crossing, it easily allowed westbound locals to get on the Pembine Sub from the SSAM tracks and continue west.

The main challenge with the purchase from UP was that unlike the Algoma Central or GB&W/FRVR purchases, this deal did not come with a stable of locomotives. Along with growing traffic elsewhere, the need for more power had WC combing the used locomotive market rounding up more SD45s along with an extensive rebuild of the existing fleet. As the WC overhauled and upgraded each SD45 they would add 1000 to the number (i.e., 6512 would become 7512).

L038 kicks up fresh snow as it passes the signboard for Eustis, MI, on the Pembine Sub. This quiet location with a classic white farmhouse will get a little quieter once WC builds Algoma Jct. and this track from Hermansville to Escanaba is removed after 110 years of use. December 29, 1996.

The SD45s so common around the WC were tough-looking locomotives. As I explained it to a few non-railfan acquaintances, using twenty-cylinder SD45s in everyday service is like driving a late 1960s muscle car to work every day. The distinctive radiator flares can be seen at the rear of the units. You can also see how the angle of the graphic on the nose matches up with the angle of the radiator. I believe this is one of the reasons the WC paint scheme was so striking on this model. WC 7502 leads SORE1 on October 4, 1998 at Goose Lake.

Opposite page: To get the most out of their combined properties in Escanaba, WC built a brand-new junction and connection between the old Soo Line main and the old C&NW yard at the west end of town. Algoma Jct. joined the ex-C&NW mainline at milepost 113.16 to what was deemed milepost 335.5 of the ex-SOO mileage across the Upper Peninsula. WC 6532 leads a local train out of Gladstone around the west leg of the newly constructed wye. The east leg connection can be seen at right as a picturesque stream flows through the center of the junction. July 2, 1999.

With the new route, traffic off the L'Anse Sub would make a right turn at Negaunee to head for the Ore Sub. Although it is joint track from Euclid Yard to Partridge Jct., the busy portion of the LS&I is reached here at Eagle Mills Jct. WC 6627 east is approaching the CTC signal and switch just ahead. At right, the track with a coating of iron ore pellets is the busy route to Eagle Mills and the Presque Isle dock. September 6, 1998.

The ore car fleet continued to run in the C&NW colors and numbers for a few years under WC ownership. In time, all the cars were cycled through the shop receiving a roller bearing retrofit of the friction bearing trucks, new reporting mark and number, along with a quick shot of maroon paint. A close look at an SSAM car clearly shows its heritage in the form C&NW's "ball and bar" logo ghosting through. February 17, 2002.

Opposite page: With the Union Pacific purchase, WC became the sole outside connection for the Lake Superior & Ishpeming, meaning a steady movement of freight to supply the mining industry and their manufacture of iron ore pellets. L045 out of Escanaba has worked the siding at Queens and is making the short hop to Eagle Mills Yard as the conductor rides the rear car. The covered hoppers that dominate this train carry bentonite clay, a staple of these general freights and a binder for making ore pellets. September 6, 1998.

800-424-9300
PPGX 3396
CAPY 16645 GALS
CAPY 63008 L

A new route from the Marquette Range to Escanaba meant the end of railroading in downtown Marquette after 140 years. WC moved its crew base in the area to Euclid Yard in Ishpeming once the deal closed on the Union Pacific tracks. Although the heyday of railroading in Marquette happened years before the WC, evidence of its history remained: the roundhouse, lower yard stretching along the lake, the monolithic ore dock, the towering approach trestle curving between the rooftops, and multiple depots. At 3rd St in Marquette, we can see where the mainline crossed under the ore dock approach. In the distance is the large sandstone depot and former headquarters of the DSS&A, in private ownership and converted to offices years before WC's presence in Marquette. The rails are silent but there are big changes on the way. WC would remove the track here and the approach trestle as well. The bridge girders of the approach would be used to upgrade wooden trestles elsewhere, notably on the Superior Sub. The prime real estate at lower yard would be sold off and redeveloped. November 29, 1997.

Opposite page:

Above: It is an arctic blast with a -15-degree air temperature at daybreak in Marquette. A crew is on duty to run a plow train. SDL39 585 is already out of the roundhouse and waiting on the lead. A backhoe has been used to move Jordan spreader 315 out of the roundhouse as well and onto the turntable. As the sun rises over the horizon, 315 is spun so it can be paired up with the locomotive ahead of the day's work. December 26, 1996.

Below: After the WC abandoned the line through Marquette, the roundhouse was razed. Little was left on September 5, 1998, a yellow Soo Line box and the turntable resting on bare ground. Marquette would rapidly change in the years after WC ceased to be a presence. In twenty years, UP Health System–Marquette would construct a new hospital on this site.

The old DSS&A to Munising Jct. was surplus once traffic was redirected down the Ore Sub to Escanaba. Munising would continue to be served from the east. Locations such as Au Train fell silent for a few years until this route was converted into a snowmobile trail. In time, a replica depot trailhead building would be constructed here. November 29, 1997.

The challenging run up Marquette Hill was eliminated by the Ore Sub acquisition. The weeds were taking over on September 6, 1998. Pine Hill Quarry can be seen in the distance where this track parallels the LS&I. From Pine Hill to the connection at Diamond Jct. these tracks were left in place as LS&I considered putting in a connection at Pine Hill that would allow empty trains to bypass the slow trip over their scale. Continuing through Diamond Jct. to Eagle Mills Jct. trains could go right back to the mine bypassing Eagle Mills Yard as well. An interesting idea, but twenty-five years later no further action has been taken.

C&NW's ore line gained a measure of fame during the 1980s as the stomping grounds for their ex-Norfolk & Western ALCO C628 locomotives. The area of Goose Lake has remained iconic through the decades of change following the reign of the ALCOs. It is hard to think of a better place to feature a tidy pair of SD45s and 108 ex-C&NW ore cars than snaking along the shore of Goose Lake. November 26, 1997.

SORE2 crosses Goose Lake on the Ore Sub. Limestone is a key ingredient in making iron ore pellets. The needed limestone was backhauled in ore cars from the dock at Escanaba up to the mine. Once empty, the cars would be loaded with ore pellets for the trip back south (railroad east). September 5, 1998.

Vast stretches along the middle section of the Ore Sub are flat and swampy with miles of tangent track but the terrain changes west of Little Lake. Skirting the grounds of the shuttered K. I. Sawyer Air Force Base, sandy, pine-covered hills are negotiated with some sweeping curves. WC 6528 west brings a cut of general freight to the Marquette Range on the front of an empty ore train. March 22, 1997.

WC trains could be dazzling in the fall. Their colors provided an excellent complement to the autumn foliage. This was especially true once the ore car fleet had been repainted into the maroon that matched the locomotives. SORE1 is only a couple miles into its return trip from Partridge Siding to Escanaba and is at the east end of Goose Lake. The bridge under the first car spans Goose Lake Outlet, a tributary of the East Branch of the Escanaba River. At the other end of this train's run, it will cross this drainage again just before the Escanaba River empties out into Little Bay de Noc. October 2, 2001.

This sign featuring a WC shield and an SSAM shield greeted crews as they started their trip on the Ore Sub departing the Ore Dock yard. The opposite side had a welcome back message. There was an uncommon amount of collaboration between managers and crews on the WC, usually evident by talking to WC employees but also through signage such as this. September 5, 1998.

Despite being in Wisconsin, the mill at Niagara only had rail access from the Upper Peninsula of Michigan. A branch dropped south from Quinnesec, MI, and crossed the Menominee River just upstream from Little Quinnesec Falls which provided hydro power to the paper mill. From the bridge the branch curved down a grade carved into a bluff, the mill tracks were reached via a switchback at the base of the hill. WC 3018 is seen at the bottom of the grade in Niagara on September 7, 1998.

With a couple steady customers located just south of Hayward, C&NW retained the track from a new junction with WC to Hayward after they sold the bulk of their northwest Wisconsin track to WC. Union Pacific too served Hayward via this isolated branch for a couple of years after acquiring the C&NW in 1995. Eventually UP struck a deal to sell WC their isolated switching "islands" here at Hayward and the remnant in and around Wausau. With the conductor riding the rear steps WC 7505 switches at Hayward on October 11, 1998.

The track arrangement at Hayward meant trains would shove backwards the 4 miles to Hayward Jct. To protect this long shove across a handful of crossings a caboose was assigned to this job. The conductor would ride the rear platform and signal with a trainline air whistle as needed. WC 18 is an ex-AC caboose at Hayward on October 11, 1998. 18 is one of the Algoma Central cars that had not been modified for remote control service and retains much of its original appearance aside from plating over the side and cupola windows.

8

CN HAULAGE TRAINS MOVE FROM BNSF TO WC

Canadian National changed from being government owned to a private carrier in 1995. Far from a mere formality, this move foretold a reexamining of what the strengths and weaknesses of the network were and what the future could hold.

BUILDING THE NAFTA RAILWAY

The Duluth, Winnipeg & Pacific had long been the CN-owned connection into the northern Midwest. As traffic steadily grew, the CN looked to Burlington Northern for haulage rights where whole trains could be handed off at Superior for forwarding to Chicago (similar to an earlier agreement in the 1980s that saw CN trains off the DW&P handled by Milwaukee Road to Chicago). The arrangement worked well but steady growth meant CN had hit the ceiling of what BN, later BNSF, could and would handle each day. As the CN continued to grow in profitability, they made the bold move of taking control the Illinois Central in early 1998. Putting together a "NAFTA railway" to take advantage of new trading patterns between Canada, the U.S., and Mexico meant the north–south flow of CN traffic to Chicago would continue to grow.

With the moves that WC made to overcome the obstacles to overhead traffic and improvements made to the Superior–Chicago route, they were an obvious choice for CN's haulage trains to Chicago. By the fall of 1998, CN's haulage trains had moved from the BNSF to WC. In 1999, CN fully merged the IC operations into their own. Rather than simply getting trains to Chicago connections and their own Grand Trunk Western Railroad, CN would be routing traffic directly to the central and southern Midwest.

CN trains would be a major part of the traffic mix along the WC mainline for the last three years of its independence. They also foretold the future of the WC routes.

CN train 346 departs Stevens Point on February 17, 2001. This control point was established in the late 1950s. Prior to that time, there was only a single-track bridge across the Plover River at the east end of the yard. In the coming years, more capacity would be added with multiple tracks continuing east another couple miles.

CN operations in the U.S. were hardly anything new given their long-time subsidiaries Duluth, Winnipeg & Pacific, Grand Trunk Western, and Central Vermont. It was, however, a new look for WC territory as CN haulage trains became a larger part of the traffic mix. The heart of tiny Conrath, WI, is the post office which sits next to the Superior Sub. Many times a day, long trains rumble through town at track speed. An SD40-2 in CN's "North America" paint scheme leads CN train 347 towards Superior. The flag, post office, and map on the locomotive all allude to the international corridor the WC mainline was rapidly becoming. December 27, 1999.

Long-distance intermodal was a big part of CN's business strategy. Expediting long trains of double stacks between Chicago and western Canada made use of WC's mainline as seen here crossing the Valley Sub at Junction City. A trio of EMDs from CN and GTW power train 377 on April 5, 1998.

CN had plenty of traffic to send over the WC, but the big trains normally had an adequate amount of modern power on them. A couple of GE Dash 9 locomotives head west into the setting sun on train 341 at Hewitt, WI, on September 7, 1998. The four-window safety cab was a look specific to CN locomotives from the 1970s into the 1990s.

Stevens Point seemed to be a perpetually busy place, especially once the CN haulage trains were part of the mix. The nature of this yard as a hub for central Wisconsin traffic is evident in the wall of pulpwood cars visible on the yard lead behind departing train 348. With a fresh crew CN 2620 is headed for Shops Yard and points east on September 29, 2001.

CN train 346 runs east over the Neenah Sub crossing the Tomorrow River at Amherst, WI. Within a mile of here, the Tomorrow River combines with Bear Creek to form the Waupaca River. In the Menominee language, Wāpahkoh (Waupaca) means tomorrow. The Menominee named the river Waupaca as it took them twenty-four hours to traverse from one end to the other. In twenty-four hours, train 346 is likely to be in Chicago on CN's Illinois Central. February 17, 2001.

9

TRAINS AND TRAFFIC:
Double Track, Detours and Commodities

By the close of the 1990s WC had grown its network through acquisition and consolidation, there was more tonnage and train traffic than the Superior–Chicago route had ever seen. To keep up with the growth WC invested in capacity improvements.

SOUPING UP THE SUPERIOR SUB

The Superior Sub (from Ladysmith to Superior) was one of the last pieces of major construction by the independent original Wisconsin Central in 1908. While built to the "modern" standard, it never carried the same amount of tonnage as the line to Minneapolis or the mainline through central and southern Wisconsin. To accommodate the traffic attracted by the modern WC, sidings needed to be extended and new ones built; later, automated switches were installed and eventually centralized traffic control.

BATTLING BYRON HILL

In southeast Wisconsin, there was another challenge, one that had bedeviled the Soo Line for many years. The climb out of the Lake Winnebago basin is known as Byron Hill. While there were steeper grades to be found in scattered corners of the railroad, none of them saw the constant parade of heavily loaded, and long, southbound trains encountering Byron Hill. If there was any positive to be found in the location of this hill, it was how close it is to Shops Yard. A helper engine and crew can be ready around the clock and do other tasks in the meantime. It is also a good stress test for any power fresh out of the shop: if it's capable of lifting a train up the hill to Byron, it should have smooth sailing the rest of the way to Chicago. When power was not up to the challenge, it was not uncommon to see an ailing train swap an engine or two with a northbound nearing the end of their run. Even with helpers, climbing the hill could be a slow ordeal. Although tantalizingly close to home, northbound trains

WC train T048 bound for Belt Railway's Clearing Yard in Chicago approaches the crest of Byron Hill lead by run-through Conrail locomotives. One of WC's more ambitious projects, the doubletracking of Byron Hill is well underway in this photo. The popular view from County Highway F was first transformed by the removal of many trees that had been steadily encroaching upon the tracks, then by earthmoving to widen the cut, grading for the second track until finally the second track was built. November 11, 1998.

Near the bottom of Byron Hill, the mainline crosses the East Branch of the Fond du Lac River. The original concrete arch bridge can be seen augmented by newer concrete. In three years, the bridge would be built up even more with two large culverts and more fill to allow the installation of a second main track through here. An SD45 and F45 are pushers on the rear of an eastbound freight about to ascend Byron Hill. September 30, 1995.

could be in for a long wait at the top while the opposition struggled against gravity. Plenty of trains would run afoul of their hours of service and expire at twelve hours on duty before reaching Shops Yard. This earned Valley Siding at the bottom of the hill the grim nickname "Death Valley" for its propensity to collect crewless trains when crews had to be taxied back to the terminal.

Despite all the other improvements made to the trunk of the WC, Byron Hill remained the obstacle it had always been. With the ongoing boom in traffic, it was decided to do something to ease this bottleneck. WC started an ambitious project to double track the hill by constructing new a track to connect the east end of Valley Siding with the west end of Byron Siding. Building a second main track was substantial undertaking. There are plenty of places where a mainline has been reduced from two tracks to one in the last 100 years, but there was never more than a single track up the hill. All the grading had to be done from scratch along with an expansion of the existing concrete arch bridge over the East Branch of the Fond du Lac River. Once completed, the popular photographer vistas on the hill were transformed and heavy traffic on the Chicago Sub became more fluid as northbound traffic could ease down the hill at the same time southbound moves slowly climbed up.

DETOURS

Given the geographic position of the WC between major terminals of the CP and BNSF in Minnesota and Chicago, it served as an emergency detour route for them and other railroads at various times. Conversely, there would be times WC had to run their own detours across Wisconsin using novel routings.

Historically, a lot of East Coast traffic, both freight and passenger, crossed Upper Michigan to Sault Ste. Marie continuing the rest of the way via Canadian Pacific. This routing explained CP's majority stake in the DSS&A and Soo Line for most of their existence. More recently, that traffic was minimal once cross-border containers moved from this gateway to lower Michigan. There were, however, occasions when disruptions on the CP mainline north of Lake Superior would send detour trains over the WC, through Sault Ste. Marie to Sudbury, Ontario, back onto the CP mainline.

The darkest hour of the Wisconsin Central's history began before dawn on March 4, 1996. An eastbound WC train was passing through Weyauwega, WI, when it derailed at speed starting with the seventeenth car; thirty-seven cars derailed in total. Derailed cars of LPG and propane ignited upon impact, spreading to a trackside feed mill in a dangerous inferno that would burn for over two weeks. All residents of the town and nearby areas were evacuated for sixteen days, and the cause was ultimately determined to be a broken switch component. The undetected bolt-hole fractures brought FRA scrutiny across the railroad and the derailment ultimately cost the WC $28 million. Located near the heart of WC's network, ongoing operations were challenged at the same time emergency management was in full swing. The railroad was nearly split in two and several detour routes were required, some using all WC track, others using combinations of their own and competitors tracks. Not far away was the roughly parallel GB&W; unfortunately, it was severed by 1996, so the detours would need to be more elaborate and circuitous to keep the traffic flowing.

There were occasions through years when CP Rail availed themselves of the original SOO mainline to detour train trains that would otherwise go around the top of Lake Superior, when that route suffered a blockage. Using the route through Sault Ste. Marie and the former CP, now Huron Central line, to Sudbury they would reconnect with their trans-Canada mainline. A pair of CP SD40-2s head up an eastbound detour train at the pulpwood siding of Ensign east of Rapid River, MI. January 18, 1997.

One of many detour trains operated in the wake of the Weyauwega derailment was this empty train of steel hoppers headed back to Superior and the DM&IR for ore loading. This train detoured westbound over CP Rail to New Lisbon where it headed up the Valley Sub. The setting sun glints off the sides of the uniform cars just north of Rudolph, WI. Up ahead is Junction City where the train will resume its normal routing on the Superior Sub. EMD 1565 was an ex-Norfolk & Western SD35 leased by WC. The high-hood SD35s earned the nickname "bricks." March 9, 1996.

Despite a connection with CP Rail at New Lisbon, there were never any regular WC trains at the south end of the Valley Sub. When CP had the contract to operate coal trains to the Weston power plant, they would run up the Valley Sub from New Lisbon with CP crews. That made the Weyauwega detour trains an especially rare catch. One of those trains was this loaded ore train from the DM&IR. WC 6577 is swinging off the Valley Sub onto the CP mainline headed towards Portage and Duplainville. March 9, 1996.

WC 6651 east is crossing over the Duplainville diamond on the CP mainline. This Weyauwega detour train is nearing the end of its reroute on CP from New Lisbon. Once over the diamond and clear of the crossover switch, it will back through the crossover and the northeast connection onto the WC Chicago Sub. March 8, 1996.

WC 6630 with another detour train has been following WC 6651 before coming to a stop short of the home signals for Duplainville. Given the location of the Weyauwega derailment at the heart of the railroad a lot of trains had to detour, often in small fleets. Once WC 6651 crosses the CP diamonds headed for Chicago, WC 6630 will get the line-up eastbound and make the same moves as the prior train. March 8, 1996.

Clattering across the same diamond in the other direction WC 6651 is back on WC rails resuming its normal route to Chicago. The connection between the two railroads here was installed by Soo Line after the purchase of the Milwaukee Road. It allowed them to integrate the two operations in this area. Later WC ran a daily train to interchange with SOO/CP at Milwaukee using the connection. In the CN era, the connection fell into disuse and by the twentieth anniversary of CN ownership had been removed entirely. March 8, 1996.

The Weyauwega derailment did not just displace WC trains onto other railroads, it also bumped through traffic onto some secondary lines. On this morning, the Shawano Sub saw a fleet of three trains: a detouring Superior-bound manifest, a detouring Superior-bound ore empty (seen here), and train T011. T011 was the only regular train through here and all three were radio blocking with each other on about a 30-minute headway. The ore empty is crossing the Wolf River at Ninemile Rapids near Hollister, WI. The following year this line was made redundant as a through route by the purchase of the Union Pacific north of Green Bay. March 16, 1996.

A detouring ore train has just started its trip down the Valley Sub at sunset. Just to the right of the lead motor, a fixed approach semaphore blade can be seen warning of the crossing of the Superior Sub in Junction City. Winter and spring open more vistas when the previous years corn has been harvested and new growth has not yet taken over. March 16, 1996.

The WC mainline between Minneapolis and Chicago was longer than either the BNSF or CP route between those points, but when rivers, particularly the Mississippi, overflowed their banks, the WC provided a welcome respite. A snowy, cold, and lingering winter followed by a rapid spring warm-up created a flood crest that disrupted operations along the Upper Mississippi in April 1997. Being among the busiest corridors in the upper Midwest meant a lot of trains needed to detour onto other routings and other railroads including the WC. In addition to the BNSF and CP detours were the overhead CN trains that would normally be on BNSF tracks.

In the spring of 1997, there was extensive flooding along the Upper Mississippi River impacting both the CP and BNSF mainlines. Both railroads turned to WC for alternate routings to move trains between Minnesota and Chicago. BNSF 991 east is a detour train out of Minneapolis passing the depot at Stanley, WI. April 13, 1997.

Opposite page:

Above: During the 1997 floods, CP Rail ran several detours using their own tracks as far as New Lisbon, the WC Valley Sub up to South Necedah, and the UP Adams Line west to the Twin Cities. The UP-WC connection at Necedah is made by means of a loop track that allows trains from Adams yard to curve around and under their own track as they head towards Wisconsin Rapids on the Valley Sub. With CP trains travelling in the other direction on both lines, backing trains around the loop would be necessary. To keep the detours flowing smoothly during this unusual move CP stationed SOO GP38-2 4417 and a crew at South Necedah to couple onto the rear of detouring trains and guide them around the loop onto the UP and *vice versa*. During a spring snow squall the 4417 backs onto the end of detouring train 425 on April 12, 1997.

Below: An eastbound CP flood detour train has just about completed its backwards transit of the Necedah loop. Momentarily the crewman will step off the 6410 and line up train 204 onto their route south down the Valley Sub for New Lisbon and home rails. The 1996 Weyauwega detours and 1997 flood detours provided a temporary jump in tonnage between South Necedah and New Lisbon that it had not seen in decades. At one time, the bottom end of the Valley Line and New Lisbon was a hub where the Milwaukee Road funneled its central Wisconsin traffic onto the mainline. It was a key detour connection, otherwise one of the quietest corners of the WC. April 13, 1997.

It was always interesting to see Soo Line locomotives back in the old "home" territory. Of course, in this case, 6049 was not built until two years after WC started up, so it was not quite the reunion it may have seemed at first glance. This flood detour is charging west out of Auburndale on April 13, 1997.

As night falls, a BNSF flood detour hustles west just north of Duplainville. Given the volume of traffic displaced by the floods on both BNSF and CP these detours ran around the clock on both WC and UP across Wisconsin, and a combination of those routes. April 14, 1997.

It is interesting what a novelty the CN flood detour trains on WC were at the time. I made a point of capturing them on the mainline and the Valley Sub. Case in point, CN 9483 west heading down the siding at Marshfield. Ironically CN trains would be a regular sight a couple years later with their traffic routed over the WC, five years later, they would own it all. Instead, it was the landscape of Marshfield that would change dramatically. A major road project would see downtown Marshfield reshaped. The depot would be moved away from the tracks and renovated for use as a restaurant. The siding would be eliminated and this whole area transformed by the construction of the Veteran's Parkway across town parallel to the mainline. April 13, 1997.

The third crossing of the Fox River by the Chicago Sub is located south of Burlington where the mainline employs this through truss bridge. The Fox River Valley Railroad/Fox Valley & Western namesake was another significant river crossed by WC flowing from central Wisconsin into Green Bay. Like the "southern" Fox River this southbound hopper train of iron ore pellets flows towards Illinois on August 5, 1995. All-rail movements of iron ore would become a large percentage of the tonnage on the WC.

The sun has just come up at Burlington, WI, as T042 traces the edge of the White River just upstream from its junction with the Fox River. In the foreground is Echo Lake Dam. April 5, 1996.

WC train T002 approaches the west end of Shops Yard at Subway Rd. This train and its counterpart T001 ran across the center of the WC system connecting the railroads two major hubs, Steven Point and Shops Yard (North Fond du Lac). August 24, 1996.

Byron, WI, is a quintessential southern Wisconsin crossroads with a town hall, feed mill, bar, and a handful of homes. Its real notoriety is among railroaders who work the hill and photographers who record the struggle. On April 6, 1996, WC 6593 leads an eastbound loaded ore train stopped on the siding short of the Highway 175 crossing. When its westbound opposition arrives, it will pull the rest of the way into the siding to allow the westbound to proceed down the hill.

WC 6613 brings a loaded Minorca–Escanaba ore train XOSTES-3 east on the Pembine Sub mainline at Dunbar, WI. On the siding, a borrowed Conrail SD50, 6706 leads an empty train waiting for the passage of the loads so it can resume its westward journey across northern Wisconsin. February 5, 2000.

WC decided to try something different with the Minorca–Escanaba trains in the winter season of 2000–2001. A selection of WC power was traded with CSX for the use of ten ex-Conrail SD80MACs. The idea was to use their distributed power capability to have a locomotive on each end of the train to control pull-aparts. The visitors met with some success but also had challenges and were not used in subsequent years. An example of the difficulties that could be had with the SD80MACs is seen on January 27, 2001. CSX 0804 was running solo on an empty train but shut down unexpectedly a couple miles east of Tripoli, WI. After a long cold wait, the crew had to hike out across a snowy field to be cabbed to their hotel. A fresh crew that had expected to take this train from Prentice to Superior was waiting 18 miles away. An alternate plan was hatched. The Superior crew was cabbed up to Park Falls to grab a unit off train L015, then run it down to Prentice and over to the dead ore train. It was dark by the time they reached the train. The SD80MAC was moved to a crossing at Tripoli where a mechanic from Stevens Point worked on reviving the beast without any luck. By the next morning, CSX 0804 was shipped out on L016 back towards Stevens Point.

Oshkosh Truck in their namesake city was a long-standing shipper for WC as it had been for Soo Line. At Waukesha, a pair of M1070 trucks, built for the U.S. Army as heavy equipment transporters, pass through on a WC flatcar as part of train T050. These 700-horsepower trucks were designed to pull a specialized trailer for hauling heavy equipment including M1 Abrams battle tanks. February 10, 1996.

Nearly all the iron ore production in northeastern Minnesota was pelletized by the 1990s. The exception was natural ore from the stockpile at the Auburn Mine. Natural ore was problematic to run through the docks and unload from ships so "all-rail" moves over the WC to U.S. Steel in Gary, Indiana, became a semi-regular move across Wisconsin. Like the old C&NW ore cars, this made for trains that were short, heavy, and brittle with plenty of slack action. Bad ordered cars were a common sight on various set-out tracks along the route of the all-rails, such as this natural ore load with a broken yoke. This Missabe car would cool its heels here at Theresa Station, WI, until a carman could visit and make the necessary repairs. November 11, 1995.

10

SPECIALS AND EXCURSIONS

WC was able to bring a certain panache to its regular operations but beyond that, finding special trains was not uncommon, either in cooperation with other operators or on their own to thank shippers or employees.

SHIPPERS, CUSTOMERS, PASSENGERS

The WC era was a great time for those looking to charter railroad excursions as well as those who wanted to watch and photograph special trains. In addition to outside groups, the WC themselves hosted many trains for customers and other stakeholders.

In the 1980s, Quad Graphics was a successful and rapidly growing printing company in southeastern Wisconsin. The high-volume web press printing they specialized in meant railroad delivery of large rolls of coated paper stock was important to the Quad facilities. Among other plants, three Quad facilities dotted the WC Chicago Sub at Pewaukee, Sussex, and Lomira. In addition to the boxcars of paper parked behind each plant, the unexpected sight of four stainless steel private passenger cars could also be seen. Quad Graphics was rightfully proud of their modern plants, regularly entertained customers, and worked to woo new business. The Quad cars were used by employees and guests. There was even a baggage car that had been converted for use as a dance floor/night club. One of the uses was to assist Quad in providing tours of the plants along the line. They would arrange for the WC to send an engine and crew to Lomira where cars loaded with employees and guests would travel to Sussex, enjoying the Kettle Moraine scenery, and continuing the tour at their destination.

EXCURSIONS

WC was a good partner with the organizers of excursions as well. Notably the Duluth, South Shore & Atlantic Division of the Soo Line Historical & Technical Society who organized trips in the 1990s. These trips utilized cars on loan from the Lake Superior Transportation Museum with WC power. Starting in 1995 once the restoration of Soo Line FP7 2500 was completed, it too traveled some remote stretches of the Northwoods and former DSS&A tracks.

An example of WC going all out on a special train was this one running west on May 2, 1996. The *Campaign Train for Science* was a special that brought dignitaries to the Marshfield Clinic for an event. WC would normally provide clean locomotives for special trains but this pair of GP40s got a little extra attention. Not only were they spotless but decorated with a custom logo on the noses and cabs along with name of the special on the side of the long hoods. Complete with three dome cars, the train is seen passing under Arthur Road near Slinger.

Bringing up the rear of the *Campaign Train for Science* are three of the Quad Graphics business cars, including dome Silver Chalet, then ex-GB&W business car Trempealeau River, Sierra Hotel, and Prairie Rose. The front three cars were "frequent fliers" on special trains all over the WC system. May 2, 1996.

In the mid-1960s when SOO, LS&I, and C&NW needed to relocate to a new joint routing between Negaunee and Ishpeming, MI, this large cut had to be dug. This excursion headed from Marquette to Baraga was put on by the DSS&A Division of the Soo Line Historical & Technical Society. Marquette Trainmaster Clint Jones waves from the cab of the DM&IR SD9 on this foggy morning. There were several popular excursions in the 1990s organized by this group retracing much of the remaining DSS&A lines, mostly with cars loaned from the Lake Superior Transportation Museum in Duluth. August 22, 1992.

It is a rainy summer day as a DSS&A Division excursion rolls west along the Spurr River west of Michigamme, MI. GP35 4005 led the train from Marquette to Baraga where they reversed direction and the SDL39 would lead. This picturesque route hosted the *Copper Country Limited* until 1968. August 20, 1994.

Rare miles were racked up on the excursion to Thomaston, MI, on the White Pine Sub. Thomaston was once a division point on the DSS&A complete with a depot, yard, and roundhouse. By 1995, there was only a siding where pulpwood and iron ore were loaded. WC 3007 and SOO 2500 reposition some freight cars while running around their excursion train in preparation to head west on the return trip to Marengo, WI. September 16, 1995.

The 1995 DSS&A Division trips ran on the Ashland Sub and the White Pine Sub. They also coincided with the restoration of Soo Line FP7A 2500. The gleaming streamliner brought a lot of crowds out to ride the trains or just to see this classic return to its old routes. The scene at the depot in Park Falls was reminiscent of when the Soo Line was the connection between this Northwoods town and the wider world. September 17, 1995.

The second day of the DSS&A Division excursion in 1994 featured a sunny day for the trip from Marquette to Newberry and return. SDL39 585 has Trainmaster Clint Jones at the throttle curving through the rock cuts near Onota, MI. Part of rolling out the red carpet for these trips included the stack of melodious air horns that would find their way onto the locomotives. The 585 sounded every bit as good as it looked this day. August 21, 1994.

Abutting the WC tracks at Oshkosh, WI, is the airport that hosts the annual Experimental Aircraft Association (EAA) Convention and Fly-in. It had grown into a huge international event by the time WC was serving Oshkosh. *Trains to the Planes*™ was an annual trip chartered by the 20th Century Railroad Club of Chicago utilizing Amtrak equipment for weekend day-trip excursions from Chicago Union Station over the WC to Oshkosh and back each evening.

HIGH IRON FOR RESTORED STEAM

A number of restored steam engines traveled the WC during its tenure. Milwaukee Road 261 made a trip across the WC even before its restoration. At the time, it was on loan from the National Railroad Museum in Green Bay. It was first moved from the museum grounds to the old Milwaukee Road facility at the Oakland Ave Yard in Green Bay where it was prepared for long distance travel. Once ready for the road, 261 was moved across the state in a special ferry move to Minneapolis where the balance of the work was done to make the ALCO 4-8-4 fully operational again. In 1993, 261 was ready to go and was back on the WC the very first day it left Minneapolis headed for Fond du Lac where it would pull excursions between Fond du Lac and Stevens Point. There would be many more trips over the WC in years to come including a regular engagement running special trains in connection with Burlington Wisconsin's *Chocolate City Days* each May.

It is "day one" for Milwaukee Road 261 after its restoration to operation. The ALCO 4-8-4 Northern was on loan from the National Railroad Museum in Green Bay. The 261 had been in Minneapolis for a year during its restoration. After a few last-minute tweaks, the new era of operation began with the run from Minneapolis to Withrow over CP's Withrow Sub. Seen on WC rails at May Ave, it has just run the first two miles of thousands it would rack up running on the WC under its own steam. September 15, 1993.

On a daylong trip from Chippewa Falls to the west end of the WC and back, SOO 1003 rolls east high above the St. Croix River on the Arcola Bridge. This trip, not long after the restoration of the locomotive garnered a lot of attention, and for good reason, the return of Soo Line steam to perhaps the Soo Line's most iconic structure was an impressive sight. September 21, 1997.

Another nicely restored Soo Line steamer became available for trips on the WC in the late 1990s. SOO 2719 was donated to the City of Eau Claire in 1960 and restored by the Locomotive and Tower Preservation Fund starting in 1996. In October 2000, it hauled a couple weekend excursions over the west end of the Whitehall Sub (ex-GB&W). After a stop at Dodge, WI, on October 8, 2000, the ALCO 4-6-2 Pacific puts on a good show getting back underway for East Winona, WI. October 8, 2000.

WC was a friendly host to steam from out of the area as well. St. Louis and San Francisco 1522 was restored in St. Louis and was looking for a friendly railroad to test the newly rebuilt locomotive. WC had not yet been in business for a year but welcomed the Baldwin 4-8-2 for tests pulling freight and then passenger excursions on their mainline in 1988. The trips were organized by the 20th Century Railroad Club and dubbed *Up the Track to Fond du Lac*. Power that was native to the mainlines of the WC would travel the regional in the 1990s. SOO 1003, an ALCO 2-8-2, had been under restoration since the 1970s. In 1997, 1003 was able to pull excursions and did so in grand fashion on its old home rails. In 1998, another historic Soo Line steamer, SOO 2719, an ALCO 4-6-2 returned to active status following a relatively swift restoration over the previous couple years. It made a fine sight travelling around the WC with excursions, including visits to some areas for the first time, such as the west end of the ex-GB&W.

PRIVATE CHARTERS

Other groups such as the American Association of Private Railroad Car Owners (AAPRCO) also worked with the WC to host special trips. This association of individuals with a wide variety of cars put together trips to travel rare milage routes far beyond what's available with an Amtrak ticket. While not available for day trips the AAPRCO trips provide a splash of color in places that have not seen "varnish" in several generations. Trips such as the *Northwoods Explorer* racked up rare miles all over the north end of the WC, including an ultra-rare run west over the old DSS&A mainline from Nestoria to Sidnaw where the train was handed off to the Escanaba & Lake Superior for the trip up to Ontonagon. The Sidnaw Sub had never seen regular service under WC and the excursion was the last train before the tracks were sold to E&LS.

Great Lakes Western Rail Tours had a fleet of passenger excursion equipment (in C&NW yellow and green) that saw use on various trips around the WC in the 1990s and the cars were stored on the WC when not in use. They partnered with the 20th Century Railroad Club to raise money for the East Troy Electric Railroad Museum. Perhaps the most unusual interchange partner of the WC was at Mukwonago with the East Troy Electric Railroad running out to East Troy, a remnant of the once-vast Milwaukee Electric Railway and Light Company. The line was to be abandoned in 1939 when the village of East Troy purchased this segment. The village operated the line to serve freight customers until 1985 when it asked the Wisconsin Electric Railway Historical Society to operate the railroad (they had been operating over the line since 1967 under a trackage rights agreement). The money raised by the *Train to the Trolleys*™ helped the museum complete the purchase of the equipment and right-of-way.

MUSEUM TRAINS

In addition to the occasional passenger moves around the system, WC hosted a more permanent operation on the Dresser Sub. In the early 1990s, the Minnesota Transportation Museum's trains were losing their operating base of Stillwater, MN, on the ex-BN Stillwater branch. In trying to find a suitable route somewhat nearby, they looked at the stubbed ex-SOO route. At that time the only regular traffic on the line was the Amery local (L068), running twice a week out of New Brighton, MN. Seasonally, Soo Line ballast trains ran over the Dresser Sub to the quarry just north of Dresser, WI. SOO trackage rights to Dresser were part of the sale to WC. The quarry is the source of "Dresser traprock" a hard, durable, dark grey ballast seen all over the Soo Line. The light traffic combined with a depot in Osceola, WI, and the scenic route through the St. Croix River valley made the Dresser Sub a natural choice for the museum trains.

With a lease secured, the museum set up a summer base of operations at the Osceola depot running trains east to Dresser and west to Marine, MN. The new operation was christened the Osceola & St. Croix Valley Railway. An early star of the show was the Northern Pacific ALCO 10-wheeler 328. 328 would later go on static display in St. Paul pending major boiler mainte- nance. Despite this being ex-Soo Line track, the 328 was at home in the St. Croix Valley having worked NP branch lines in the area to destinations such as Taylors Falls, MN, and Grantsburg, WI. In 1998, MTM would buy a locomotive from WC to power trains on the Dresser Sub. WC 4159 was a GP7 that came with the FRVR purchase and would be repainted as "SOO 559" really MNTX 559, wearing the classic Soo Line maroon and gold from the 1950s. Originally a Rock Island locomotive, number 559 was chosen as the next number above the locomotives Soo Line had in their passenger fleet.

Opposite page: The greatest number of movements over the Dresser Sub would be operated by the Minnesota Transportation Museum's Osceola & St. Croix Valley operation. In the early years after the move to Osceola, MTM's SW1200 NP 105 was the main workhorse on these trains. The west end of normal passenger operations was Marine, MN. Shortly after running around its train at Marine NP 105 crosses over Ostrum Trail North where it tunnels beneath the WC. September 17, 1994.

NORTHERN
105

This handsome ten-wheeler ran around Minnesota quite a bit in the 1980s and 1990s. Its last regular runs were on the Osceola & St. Croix. While it is owned by the City of Stillwater, it is on long term loan to the Minnesota Transportation Museum and has been stored at their facility in St. Paul for a couple decades in need of boiler work. Back on August 6, 1994 328 was in fine form as it pulled a pair of coaches out of Osceola headed for Dresser.

WC 3027 (AC 191) was one of the last additions to the Algoma Central roster before the WC purchase. This former Milwaukee Road GP40 wore nearly new Algoma Central paint during its first years on the WC before being repainted into the unique tenth anniversary "flag" scheme. On August 24, 1995, 3027 west is pulling a business car move featuring the Sierra Hotel just past Vernon on the Chicago Sub. I presume the boxcar is on this train as a buffer to put some distance between the 3027's horns and guests in the dome.

WC ran a special train to commemorate the end of street running in Oshkosh. Two GP40s and two heavyweight passenger cars were used for the occasion. A substantial overnight snowstorm impacted the operation of the special and many other trains. Delays meant dusk was taking hold by the time this train was turned loose on Chicago Sub traversing the Kettle Moraine landscape. January 27, 1996.

One of the longest-running special trains in Wisconsin is the Great Circus Train. The Great Circus Train was used to transport a train of historic circus wagons from the Circus World Museum in Baraboo, WI, to Milwaukee once a year starting in the early 1960s. Over the years, it traveled various routes and used a wide variety of locomotives to haul the train. In 1996, Wisconsin & Southern brought the train to Milwaukee for the Great Circus Parade pulled by their E9s. A small crowd has gathered at the west end of the Waukesha yard to watch the special pass on the WC heading to Rugby Jct. where it will return to WSOR rails for the remainder of the trip to Milwaukee. July 8, 1996.

11

REBUILT LOCOMOTIVES AND CARS FROM THE WC SHOPS

With the purchase of the Lake States Transportation Division, Wisconsin Central gained very capable shops at Fond du Lac and Stevens Point. Soo Line had constructed their own freight cars as well as major overhauls and painting of locomotives. The shops continued to produce top notch work on rolling stock and motive power under Wisconsin Central.

APPLYING THE WC IMAGE

As a startup, odds are that the first WC locomotive most folks saw would be in the well-worn colors of a previous owner, with a patch underneath the cab window and two initials stenciled at the center of the patch, an upside-down M paired up with a C. Before long, however, the identity of the new WC began to emerge in full color. Similar to how the name was drawn from the history of these routes so too was the color scheme of the new carrier. The Soo Line of the 1950s was warmly remembered for the classy maroon and yellow colors applied to its road diesels. The WC livery was loosely inspired by the look of the old Soo Line, it brought plenty of good will from those who remembered the Soo Line's flagship train, *The Laker*. The shield logo was revived from the original WC yet updated to reflect the new name "Wisconsin Central Ltd." The first WC repaint featured maroon and yellow caution stripes on the nose in a chevron pattern, after that more yellow than maroon with a V-pattern, and finally the most widely applied "pine tree" pattern on the nose. On the old Soo Line scheme, a stylized pine tree in yellow was on the front of the locomotives. The WC take on this was regarded as the sun rising between two pine trees, basically an upside-down version of what Soo Line had used.

Shops Yard could be a very busy place, a lot of blocking, locals, and through trains happening around the clock. In this view an ex-SP SW1500 switches on the ex-FRVR side while ex-SOO GP30 number 713 works the ex-SOO side of the yard. SW1500s like 1557 were a common sight around the major yards. Some also had their own version of the WC paint scheme with the name imposed over a pine tree graphic. December 7, 1996.

The setting sun reflects off the clean flanks of another WC lashup pulling north alongside a marsh near Duplainville, WI. With so much power cycling through the shop plus the paint booth of the nearby Wisconsin & Southern, the 1990s were a golden era for finding great-looking trains on the Wisconsin Central. March 28, 1996.

ONE MAN'S LEMON

In another challenge to conventional wisdom, some eyebrows were raised when the new WC made SD45s the backbone of their fleet. A large group of ex-Burlington Northern units was on the market when WC was shopping for power. The high-horsepower units were only about twenty years old but had developed a mixed reputation early in their careers. The SD45 has a twenty-cylinder engine block that could flex and damage the crankshaft. Builder EMD would retrofit the engine blocks to strengthen them, but when compared to the SD40 and SD40-2 that came to dominate, the SD45 never really took off. President Edward A. Burkhardt expressed confidence in his shop forces to build a reliable fleet upon these secondhand locomotives. To address another knock on SD45s WC derated their units from 3,600 horsepower to 3,300, decreasing fuel consumption a bit. Knowing the terrain and the traffic of the railroad along with the distances, the unconventional choice of SD45s paid off for WC. The initial fleet of SD45s would be augmented through the years several more times, including a large influx off the Santa Fe when theirs became available. WC was pleased enough with the SD45s that after putting a lot of their own miles on them, they cycled many of them through the shop for a major rebuild and upgrade. To designate the units that had been through the program, the road numbers were bumped from the 6400s–6600s to the 7400s–7600s as each locomotive went back into service.

Santa Fe started to shed what had originally been a fleet of 125 SD45s by the 1990s and WC was ready to augment the SD45s already on their roster. As a first step, they got their new number and a quick WC initial on the cab. Sitting on the roundhouse whisker tracks at Gladstone two former Santa Fes bracket an ex-BN SD45 between assignments. They would each get their turn in paint shop for WC garb, but the silver trucks as seen on 6596 would turn up for years to come as a reminder of the Santa Fe heritage. July 20, 1993.

We see 6596 again after a trip to the paint shop for a fresh coat of maroon and gold, still with the slightly mismatched number boards. Lost Arrow Road marks the unofficial bottom of Byron Hill where trains start the tough climb south out of the basin of Lake Winnebago. Going track speed at this point was critical to carrying momentum up the hill as far as possible and slowly grinding it out by the time the top was reached, especially if there was no helper engine pushing from behind. Train T046 on December 7, 1996.

There were plenty of special paint schemes on the WC. Many railroads help to promote Operation Lifesaver with one or more locomotives, often slightly changing their standard livery to make room for the OLS logo. On two SD45s painted to boost Operation Lifesaver awareness, WC created elaborate paint schemes that were distinct from both the standard livery and each other. WC 7638 was one of the customized OLS engines. The design of 7638's graphics bore similarities to those worn by the F45s, particularly the large lightening bolt on the flank. Seen here crossing Goose Lake westbound with train SORE2 on the Ore Sub. October 2, 2001.

Late winter flurries are highlighted by the headlight beams of SORE2 at Little Lake, MI. This loaded ore train is headed back to Escanaba but has paused here on the mainline waiting out a meet with a northbound train headed up to the Marquette Range. Heavy trains in remote locations and all kinds of weather required reliable power to meet the challenge. WC locomotives rebuilt and maintained in their own shops performed well for the growing railroad. March 22, 1997.

EXPERIMENTS AND INNOVATIONS

The shop also worked on other initiatives. With the Algoma Central purchase came a small fleet of modern cabooses ("Pointe Ste-Charles" cars designed and built by CN at their large Montreal shop). When these cars were selected to be a part of the remote-control/one-man-operation tests WC was embarking upon, they were cycled through the shop. Modifications to the cars included headlights, horns, ditchlights, radio control gear, MU (multiple unit) connections on both ends, along with additional safety gear. In time the cars would have most of the windows plated over. There would come to be an additional need for remote cars once WC was contracted to operate limestone trains over an industrial railroad at Gulliver, MI, similarly equipped cars were built out of flatcars.

There was a steady flow of used freight cars that WC purchased, cycling through the shop to serve customers all over the railroad. Some cars had more modifications than a straight rebuild and repainting. From the beginning of the WC to the end, hauling pulpwood logs was a focus across the Northwoods. Early on, much of this traffic was moved in ex-SOO bulkhead gondolas and as they were replaced bulkhead rack flats cycled through the shops as a safer alternative to crosswise loaded gondolas. Crosswise logs had an unfortunate tendency to shift during transit until they moved far enough to topple off the top of a loaded car while in motion. The WC started to release bulkhead wood racks that were paired with a solid drawbar. The bulkheads where the cars came together were removed. With fewer parts to fail, less slack action, and a boosted capacity, these cars were christened "Mega Log-Haulers."

An innovative project undertaken by the WC was the development of cabooses to house remote control gear. The steel cupola cars came with the Algoma Central purchase. Once modified, the cars would receive radio signals from a beltpack controller and pass the control signals to whatever locomotive was connected to the caboose. No modifications to the locomotive were needed. Other modifications included an airhorn, bell, and headlights all controllable from the beltpack. These cars saw extensive testing as part of engineer only trials on the White Pine Sub. On May 10, 1996, train L044 has caboose WC-14 bracketed by WC 820 and WC 3023 as it gets underway at Marengo Jct. on its way to White Pine. After the road trials on this line the remote cabooses would see use in various yards around the railroad.

Remote-control caboose WC 11 featured many of the same modifications as WC-14 with some notable differences. WC 11 only had a headlight installed at one end of the car despite having MU connections at both ends. Coupled ahead of the caboose are a couple bulkhead flatcars WC converted for remote control operation. The flats featured indicator lights, headlights, horns, railings, air tanks, and MU connections. WC contracted with a quarry east of Gulliver to operate their limestone trains from the quarry to Port Inland on Lake Michigan. The shuttle trains made the 5-mile trip over the industrial railroad with a one-man crew and one of these converted flatcars. This allowed them to run the shuttles of side-dump cars in push-pull fashion with an SDL39 and the flatcar at the south end of each train. On the return trip, the power would be operated remotely from the north end of the train.

Another innovation from the WC shops was geared toward a major WC commodity: pulpwood. A series of ex-Southern Railway bulkhead flatcars were cycled through the shop and emerged in drawbar conjoined sets; stakes installed for lengthwise loading with the interior bulkheads removed. Originally a fleet of seventy-five was planned, but ultimately fifty of the pairings were produced. Drawbar coupled cars weren't a new idea but for these pulpwood cars the design increased the capacity by 32 percent resulting in a seventy-cord capacity car. WC 35200 is the prototype car. The rest of the cars that followed would feature "Mega Log Hauler" lettering. These cars were produced at the end of WC's independence and originally used a WCCL reporting mark. With a full load of pulp, WC 35200 is seen at Stanberry, WI, on the Superior Sub, May 31, 2005.

Still hard at work on the WC, GP30 814 had seen three owners and over three decades of service in its original C&NW colors. The years were evident in the mismatched number boards, the yellow door, the rust, dust, and scratches. After a couple years on the railroad, it was cycled through the shop for some much-needed maintenance and TLC. Seen parked between runs at CF Yard on the Minneapolis Sub, August 18, 1994.

With a new number and dressed up in DuPont Imron paint, the old 814 is seen post-makeover at Wisconsin Rapids on April 5, 1998. Other modifications from its visit to the shop can be seen such as the removal of the class lights and the addition of a pilot plow. All three ex-FRVR GP30s would cycle through the shop for similar work. WC 2251 was unique in that the lettering on the long hood is smaller and lighter than what was applied to siblings 2252 and 2253.

Given the steadily growing business on the WC, when the Algoma Central locomotives came onboard, they were put right to work. The minimal remarking the power received consisted of a WC shield on the nose and a new number. WC 1501 is a GP7R that Algoma Central had builder GMD remanufacture in 1978 (AC 100). On August 24, 1995, it is resting on the spur across from the depot at Waukesha, WI.

The ex-AC high-hood Geeps were cycled through the shop as part of an in-house rebuild program. The obvious changes were the chopped short noses and fresh application of WC colors. Many other more subtle improvements were made at the same time such as the all-weather window. On January 27, 2001, the crew from an Escanaba to Superior all-rail empty is headed south on the Ashland Sub near Fifield, WI, using WC 1501 as a "rescue" unit for a train that broke down east of Tripoli.

When WC took over the Union Pacific trackage at Wausau, WI, it comprised a few miles of trackage. The busiest piece was the remnant of a through route across the Wisconsin River to the west side of town and a spur to a 3M roofing granules plant. The spur leaving the plant is on a grade with some tight curvature posing a challenge to the heavy slow speed switching work. A variety of models from WC's eclectic roster were tried on this job. Beyond the WC roster, this MP2000C demonstrator paid a visit to the WC including a stint on the job serving 3M. On August 8, 1999, it is seen switching on the west side of Wausau near the switch leading to the plant. Boise Locomotive was the successor to Morrison-Knudsen's rail division, it was soon to merge with Westinghouse Air Brake to form Wabtec. As for the 6201, it was built on the frame and trucks of an ex-Southern Pacific SD35 with modern emissions and traction control systems. There were not any sales of MP2000Cs and 6201 would remain one of a kind until scrapped in January of 2022.

Although MPEX 6201 was returned with no orders placed by WC, it had planted the seed of an idea. The upgraded version of an SD35 was sure-footed and performed well on the challenging profile of the Wausau 3M spur. WC had an SD35 of its own, WC 2500, an oddball on the roster which came with the Fox River Valley purchase. It was conspicuous wherever it went still in its Southern Railway colors with a chopped nose. 2500 bounced around the system for years until it was sidelined by an electrical fire, not long after the 6201 had visited. WC rebuilt the 2500 with plenty of upgrades including Q-Tron electronics. The renewed 2500 got rave reviews from those who ran it and became a fixture on Wausau's 3M spur. I suspect the visit of the MPEX 6201 served as an inspiration for the rebuild of WC 2500. It would wander farther from its "assignment" after the CN takeover before ultimately leaving the roster. The 2500 was scrapped in 2020. WC 2500 was photographed at Stevens Point on February 17, 2001.

The cowl-bodied F45s garnered a lot of attention as soon as WC acquired them from the Santa Fe. Early reports indicated that the cowl units would be used for parts to sustain the SD45 fleet. Thankfully, the shop was up to the task of rehabbing and maintaining them as part of the roster. WC 6653 grinds up Byron Hill with train T142 on March 15, 1997.

One of the unique aspects of the WC F45s was their paint scheme. On half the units (6650, 6654, and 6656) porthole windows in doors near the rear of the units lined up with the road name and number in such a way that the numbers ran across the porthole. WC 6654 was on public display at Mukwonago, WI, in conjunction with the East Troy Electric Railroad on May 4, 1996. Looking out the rear porthole on the engineer's side portions of a 6 and 5 are seen on the window.

On the occasion of WC's tenth anniversary, the two GP40s acquired with the Algoma Central were repainted into commemorative paint schemes. Custom shields were developed for both units. WC 3026 featured an antique map graphic on both sides of the long hood with a "150 years and rolling" inscription to also honor the Wisconsin state sesquicentennial. WC 3027 featured the flags of each state and the province WC operated in on both sides of the long hood. In addition to special trains, the pair were run on freights together after their release from the shop. In later years, they would roam the system separately. Finding the pair at Tomahawk was appropriate given their origins on the Milwaukee Road roster. The yard here is the stub-ended upper limit of the old Valley Line. WC reached Bradley over the Tomahawk Railway from Tomahawk. November 30, 1997.

Just south of the Wausau yard, the Valley Sub crosses the Eau Claire River. Headed across the river train L012 provides a tidy summary of the origins of much of WC's fleet of late 1990s branch line power. SDL39 590 is a "day one" locomotive that has been with the railroad from the start and can trace its heritage to the Milwaukee Road like this bridge and most of the Valley Sub. GP38-2 2004 is a reliable veteran of the Algoma Central that would be repainted before the year was over. Bringing up the rear is first generation GP9 1702 older by a couple decades. 1702 represents the various locomotives that came with the Fox River Valley purchase, it is one of only a handful of units to receive FRVR's bright red and yellow paint scheme. It would wear these colors the whole time it served WC. February 6, 1999.

A batch of seven ex-Southern Railway SD45s went through the WC shop for maintenance, upgrades, and rebuilds. These were some of the heavier overhauls done to the SD45s WC acquired. As a part of their rebuild, the short hoods were lowered and the control stand repositioned into the standard placement. WC 6553 brings an eastbound train up to the top on Byron Hill (note the completed double track project) on a snowy February 4, 2003. Once painted to match the fleet, one of the spotting features were the silver-rimmed windows retrofitted above the short hood.

12

END OF THE WC ERA

What had started as the cast-off sale of an underperforming division was now seen as a key piece of a rival class one.

A PIECE OF THE CN PUZZLE

The WC had a meteoric rise and a remarkable record of growth during its existence. In time the modern and efficient railroad that had been built became too attractive as a takeover target. In the latter half of the 1990s, a bumpy series of class one mergers, such as the Union Pacific-Southern Pacific combination had resulted in service crises and legions of unhappy shippers. When a proposal to combine giants BNSF and CN was brought forward in 1999, the Surface Transportation Board put the brakes on all large-scale deals for a period of 2 years. At the end of those two years CN was ready acquire WC and secure a permanent route to Chicago from the north.

TOWARDS THE END

There had been many steps taken in the history of the WC that led towards it being a piece of the CN's future, as outlined in previous chapters. However, arguably the biggest step and sharpest indicator of what was the come was the board's removal of Edward A. Burkhardt as president and CEO in July 1999. WC seemed to be at a crossroads and there was no longer unity of direction from its leadership. It can be argued that WC was Mr. Burkhardt's finest work, and his interest was to see continued investment and growth of the WC as an independent carrier. Thomas F. Power Jr. wanted to increase income by limiting expenditures. It would seem the change in leadership coincided with a board that was amenable to the sale of the railroad. Mr. Burkhardt attempted to win back control of the board through a proxy battle in January 2001 but was unsuccessful. Only eighteen days later, CN publicized its agreement to purchase the WC.

The WC was still a successful and profitable railroad, but the ownership had diversified with significant holdings around the world in Great Brittan, New Zealand, and Australia. The international holdings were not performing as well as the core system, becoming a drag on the overall performance.

A lot of the things that made the WC stand out at the beginning had been adopted by other railroads by the time they were done, including the two-man caboose-less trains. Other aspects of the Class I competitors were now found on WC such as unionized train crews.

To a large extent, both geographically and operationally, Stevens Point was the heart of the Wisconsin Central. The large brick depot served as offices for systemwide and Western Division managers and the home of the dispatching offices. After the CN takeover Stevens Point would remain the base for customer service staff serving the old WC territory. Train NBST (New Brighton–Stevens Point) arrives at "Point" as the sun sets on February 17, 2001.

When time ran out on the independent Wisconsin Central, it was a resounding success by almost any measure. The mainline was busier than ever booming with traffic. As exciting as that can be, I decided to close out the WC years at a much slower pace, spending the last day along the Barron Sub. The original mainline of the Soo Line had withered to a pair of worn rails through the weeds hosting a short local train a few times a week. I was able to savor the end and the peak fall color although the weather was a bit somber. One of the ex-Algoma Central GP7s going the literal extra miles for small customers provided a fitting last chapter to the WC era. WC 1502 west moves at a casual 10 mph west of Weyerhaeuser, WI, on October 8, 2001.

AFTER THE END

In the weeks following WC's last day, changes were slow at first. The most unusual locomotive models were the first to be parked, especially if they were not part of a larger class of the same model on the wider CN roster. Road power from CN and IC started to make appearances on through trains along the secondary main lines. With the large fleet of SD45s, they remained a part of the mix for some years. In time, CN leased a batch of rebuilt ex-CN SD40s from locomotive rebuilder Alstrom. These were regarded as "SD45 killers" since they worked the same territory and assignments traditionally held by the WC SD45s. As if to drive home the fact, the Alstrom locomotives would be renumbered as WC 6900 series units, usually with a large white CN logo on the long hood and WC initials under the number on the cab. They would be the only locomotives acquired after the sale that would be designated WC. Eventually all the SD45s were retired and then the 6900s left as well, largely replaced by ex-UP C40-8s and former Oakway Leasing SD60s.

Local and yard power too would transform from the familiar WC fleet into one that was a mix of four-axle Geeps of Canadian National, Illinois Central, and Grand Trunk Western heritage. There were few WC locomotives retained by CN long term with only a handful, some GP40s and end cab switchers, repainted into CN colors with WC initials.

The preponderance of SD45-led trains started to diminish as the CN era progressed. Taking over the WC was not the last move CN would make in assembling its "iron lariat" around the upper Great Lakes. In a look at the future, DM&IR 205 led train NBST through New Richmond, WI, on February 23, 2002. Along with DW&P 5905, the WC and DM&IR units are indicative of the route CN built to connect itself from Chicagoland across Wisconsin and Minnesota to Canada.

Plenty of changes became official on day one, but many trains looked the same and brought the same mix of traffic over the same routes, at least initially. Policies around moving "no bill" cars changed overnight, CN would not gather loaded cars that did not yet have a waybill in the system indicating the destination of the car. It had been an element of collaboration between WC and their customers that cars could start their journey before final billing was complete. This pertained to non-hazardous lading such as pulpwood and paper. It was especially valuable to many paper mills. With rolls of paper in boxcars, mills were able to use sidetracks as extensions of their warehouses and more rapidly respond to customer orders once the destination was determined. Looking very much like the WC, an empty coke train is headed west to Roseport, MN, to be refilled. Seen at New Richmond, WI, on the Minneapolis Sub on May 10, 2002. These cross-Wisconsin unit coke trains would cease in time as CN did not renew the contract and the traffic would move on other routes to Manitowoc, making most of the trip on CP instead.

In the years after the CN takeover, WC mainline power continued to move tonnage both on the railroad and on other carriers for horsepower payback. As time went by, the SD45 fleet steadily dwindled, as failures occurred units were retired *in lieu* of repair. With this turnover, CN supplemented the roster with GEC Alsthom SD40 rebuilds. Arriving as GCFX lease units, they had been rebuilt into SD40-3s at the ex-CN GEC Alsthom Pointe-Saint-Charles shop in Montreal. GCFX 6050, 6061, and 6052 power a Minorca to Escanaba ore train headed east on the Bradley Sub at Ladysmith, WI. The train is crossing the Flambeau River on February 15, 2003.

CN would purchase the fifty GCFX units they had been leasing. Widely seen as helping to step in and finish off the WC SD45s, the SD40-3s would be the last locomotives assigned the WC reporting mark and placed in the 6900 to 6949 number series. Once purchased, they would be remarked with a large CN logo on the long hood, number on the cab, WC initials below the number and a large number on the end of the long hood. None of these units would receive a full repaint after their remarking. Ultimately the SD40-3s would serve as a stopgap until new locomotives supplemented CN's high horsepower fleet and newer second-hand locomotives were acquired for local runs. After a few short years the 6900s would be sold and leave the roster. Seen at New Richmond, WI, two years after being recorded on the Minorca train (as GCFX 6052) WC 6922 rests after powering a local. May 27, 2005.

EPILOGUE

Traffic flows on what had been the WC would continue to change over time, as existing contracts came up for renewal and renegotiation. Perks offered by WC to customers, such as temporarily "warehousing" of finished product in WC boxcars that had not yet been billed to the end user, were no longer offered. Low-margin traffic such as pulpwood and coke were de-emphasized and some moved to other carriers or trucks. Investments in the Superior to Chicago mainline continued with increasing long-distance traffic. In the wake of the WC purchase, CN would also purchase the Duluth, Missabe & Iron Range and the Elgin, Joliet & Eastern to make their "iron lariat" around the upper Great Lakes complete. CN now had a seamless traffic flow to the north and south of the WC. CN would combine several of their US units (DW&P, DM&IR, and EJ&E) into the Wisconsin Central Division, keeping the name alive on WC Division trucks and on paper if not elsewhere. One last bit of maroon and yellow was applied to a modern GE ET44AC locomotive as part of their fleet of "heritage" locomotives, number 3069.

Beyond the different operating philosophy, there were larger economic factors in play creating slack in the traditional paper making industry across Wisconsin. A transition to digital communication set off a cascade of closures and consolidations among the paper mills. Traffic that had been a mainstay of northern Wisconsin railroading was struggling. The White Pine Copper Mine in western Upper Michigan ceased mining in 1995 and eventually shuttered its refinery fifteen years later. Flash floods would damage the northern end of the Ashland Sub in 2016 and operations would be curtailed to Park Falls. In 2021, CN reached a deal to sell a cluster of lightly trafficked secondary lines and branches to the Watco corporation, almost 900 miles of track in total. Both active and inactive track, the track stretches from Tony, WI (near Ladysmith), to Goodman, WI, and Wausau to Ashland as well as the White Pine Sub and the Newberry Sub along with the Algoma Central as far north as Oba, Ont. Branches also radiate out of Appleton and Green Bay plus the Medford Sub. Farther south, the Eden spur, West Bend Sub, and Saukville line would be incorporated into Watco's existing Wisconsin Southern operation. Aside from selling much of the Plymouth Sub south of Kiel to Wisconsin Southern, this was the first time CN had sold a sizable piece of the old WC in two decades of ownership.

Besides the name living on "on paper" and in the name of the operating division comprising the old WC territory, the WC reporting mark would be used occasionally by CN on new freight cars. For instance, this brand-new 75-foot-long centerbeam flat car is one of hundreds purchased by CN in the years after taking over the WC. WC 37237 carries a load of siding at Wausau, WI, on March 12, 2005.

Detour trains on the WC division have been rare during the CN era but can happen once in a great while. On August 21, 2007, a detouring BNSF train is seen heading across the Arcola High Bridge into the setting sun. It can be argued this is the most dramatic railroad entrance to the state of Minnesota. Unfortunately, once coal and coke trains were removed from the Minneapolis Sub the sole remaining train left limited options at this landmark, often crossing at night. Trailing unit, BNSF 807, would be back again. A few years later, CN would purchase a group of these C40-8Ws. 807 would return to this route and others as CN 2165.

As the ranks of older first-generation WC locomotives were stricken from the roster CN steadily moved other four-axle power into WC territory. GP38-2s and GP40s of CN, IC, and GTW heritage started appearing across the upper Midwest. Compared to the mixed power on the large trains, an extra like CN 4710 west on the Minneapolis Sub flew the new flag with little ambiguity in CN's first full year. New Richmond, WI, June 28, 2002.

CN would become the beneficiary of all the work WC had done to streamline, modernize, and upgrade the network in the upper Midwest. Over time, the WC network would look more a part of the CN as CN power moved in, new locomotives were delivered, and WC power was moved out or retired. History and transition are evident as train A412 is seen passing through Powers, MI. There is an SD45 still hanging on while the C&NW switch stand and depot testify to the long-time importance of this junction, CN 5290 flies the flag of the new owner but has obviously been racking up the miles for decades. A couple years of Union Pacific ownership did not leave any long-term impression on the area. If you look closely, there is an outline of the C&NW logo "ghosted" on the end of the depot where the herald was before the UP took over. June 11, 2005.

Elsewhere, CN has made some serious investments in parts of the WC where they have seen a good business case for expansion. After suspending service on the Barron Sub and leasing the track to Progressive Rail's Wisconsin Northern operation, CN took back the track and completely reconstructed the line when a frac sand mining boom came to the area. On the Minneapolis Sub, CN built a brand-new auto and container facility near New Richmond, WI. An improved four-lane highway and modern bridge connecting western Wisconsin to the Twin Cities metro provided a natural link for this lucrative transload traffic. As was done earlier on Byron Hill, sidings were connected by newly constructed double track on the climb out of Superior southbound alleviating another bottleneck.

Across the board, most of the WC as we knew it continues to blend in as a keystone piece of the modern CN mega-railroad. Out at the more remote corners, the same struggle to attract enough business continues for both CN and the new operators. Although now history, the Wisconsin Central is worth studying as pivotal operation in a dynamic era when upper midwestern railroading moved from legacy carriers to the robust modern Class Is we know today.

The WC era was over, but it had provided years of scenes that nobody could have predicted. "Only on the WC" had become a common expression among photographers regarding the combinations of rare locomotives found on WC trains. For instance, I figured I was a couple decades too late to see EMD F-units expediting freight over a mainline, until encountering just that first-hand on the WC. Tack on one of the nine SDL39s in existence and you have a perfect example of that axiom. L035 at Corinne, MI, January 18, 1997. It was not a great surprise that some of the rarest locomotives on the roster were the first to go when CN took over, including all the F9s and SDL39s.

Train 142 basks in the last bit of winter sunlight at Lomira, WI, having crested Byron Hill and a subsequent hill here. Much of the trip to Chicago will be under cover of darkness. Trains and scenes such as this made the WC era a boon for photographers and anyone who wished to observe a proud railroad well-run. March 15, 1997.

INDEX